King Philip's War

WITNESS TO HISTORY

Peter Charles Hoffer and Williamjames Hull Hoffer, *Series Editors*

ALSO IN THE SERIES:

Williamjames Hull Hoffer, *The Caning of Charles Sumner: Honor, Idealism, and the Origins of the Civil War*

Tim Lehman, *Bloodshed at Little Bighorn: Sitting Bull, Custer, and the Destinies of Nations*

KING PHILIP'S WAR

Colonial Expansion, Native Resistance, and the End of Indian Sovereignty

DANIEL R. MANDELL

The Johns Hopkins University Press | *Baltimore*

© 2010 The Johns Hopkins University Press
All rights reserved. Published 2010
Printed in the United States of America on acid-free paper

9 8 7 6 5 4 3 2 1

The Johns Hopkins University Press
2715 North Charles Street
Baltimore, Maryland 21218-4363
www.press.jhu.edu

Library of Congress Cataloging-in-Publication Data

Mandell, Daniel R., 1956–
   King Philip's War : colonial expansion, native resistance, and the end of
Indian sovereignty / Daniel R. Mandell.
       p.   cm.
   Includes bibliographical references and index.
   ISBN-13: 978-0-8018-9627-9 (hardcover : alk. paper)
   ISBN-10: 0-8018-9627-4 (hardcover : alk. paper)
   ISBN-13: 978-0-8018-9628-6 (pbk. : alk. paper)
   ISBN-10: 0-8018-9628-2 (pbk. : alk. paper)
   1. King Philip's War, 1675–1676. 2. Wampanoag Indians—Wars.
3. New England—History—Colonial period, ca. 1600–1775. I. Title.
   E83.67.M329 2010
   973.2'4—dc22   2009046020

A catalog record for this book is available from the British Library.

Special discounts are available for bulk purchases of this book. For
 more information, please contact Special Sales at 410-516-6936 or
specialsales@press.jhu.edu.

The Johns Hopkins University Press uses environmentally friendly book
materials, including recycled text paper that is composed of at least
30 percent post-consumer waste, whenever possible. All of our book papers
are acid-free, and our jackets and covers are printed on paper with
recycled content.

For Alden Vaughan, Jim Axtell, and Neal Salisbury,
with appreciation for their scholarship and assistance along the way

CONTENTS

King Philip's War

ꭥ Prologue

ON MARCH 22, 1621, a warm, sunny spring day, Ousamequin with twenty men came unarmed to a meeting with a small band of English settlers.[1] One of those settlers described the Wampanoag sachem, whose title "the Massasoit" has since served as his name, as "a very lustie man, in his best yeares, an able body, grave of countenance, and spare of speech."[2] They met at an abandoned Wampanoag village where on the previous December 25 (after six weeks on Cape Cod) the English had established the first European settlement in the region. When Massasoit crossed the brook and entered Plymouth, he must have noticed that only a scattering of men and women stood outside their hand-hewn small, rectangular cabins—very different from his people's oval, mound-shaped wigwams—to witness his visit and show that they had survived the winter. This group probably seemed to pose little threat (particularly since he had left forty more warriors on the other side of the brook), despite the six "musketiers" who fired a volley to salute his arrival.[3]

The English military commander, Miles Standish, went with Massasoit to one of the cabins, where, as a colonist later wrote, they had placed a green rug and several cushions for the Wampanoags, who did not use chairs. Plymouth's governor William Bradford then entered the room, trailed by a drummer and a trumpeter playing (one hopes melodically) and three musketeers to impress the visitors. The two exchanged kisses of greeting before sitting down. The governor began by offering a salute of "strong water" (whiskey?) to the sachem, and Massasoit in turn "drunke a great draught which made him then sweate all the while after"—not surprisingly: this was his first experience with alcohol, for eastern North Americans did not ferment or distill beverages. Bradford then called for "a little freshe meat," which they shared. Massasoit in turn took out some tobacco that he kept in a bag attached to a necklace that marked his authority, and the two leaders "drank" (smoked) the dried leaf in the Wampanoag ceremony.[4] With these rituals complete, the two apparently quickly reached a formal agreement establishing relations between the two peoples. Perhaps it had been discussed and worked out before the meeting, as are modern diplomatic arrangements.

Massasoit promised in the treaty that "neyther he nor any of his should injure or doe hurt to any of our people" and that if this happened he would send "the offender" to the English for punishment. If any Natives took tools from the colonists, he would make sure that the items were returned, and the colonists likewise promised that "if ours did any harme" they "would doe the like." Both the Wampanoags and the Plymouth settlers promised to assist the other "if any did unjustly warre" against them and not to carry their weapons into the settlements of the other party. Massasoit promised to help the English by telling "his neighbour Confederates" of the agreement. And the colonists concluded the text of the treaty by noting that, by agreeing to these terms, "King James would esteeme of him as his friend and Alie."[5]

Although the text gave the colonists the power to adjudicate problems between individuals from the two groups, the agreement as a whole could be interpreted as an alliance or a submission. Massasoit saw this alliance as giving him new clout in his ongoing struggles with the powerful Narragansetts and extending his endangered authority in the region. The English colonists, on the other hand, felt that Massasoit had submitted to King James and English sovereignty. The two peoples also had very different contexts for and understandings of this agreement. The English saw a formal treaty that, as in the European tradition of diplomacy, bound the signatories, their successors, and their peoples in perpetuity. Massasoit did not speak English, and Native Americans had no experience with written treaties; instead, they reached agreements that were maintained by trade, councils, and other frequent meetings and that were remembered with the assistance of designs woven into wampum—strings of hand-drilled pieces of whelk shell and clamshell beads.[6]

Over the next forty years, the numbers and power of the English newcomers would wax while those of the Natives waned. Tribal leaders continued to seek ways to maintain or expand their influence but increasingly were forced to deal primarily with the English for trade, alliances, and other economic, political, and social adjustments. On their side, colonial leaders maneuvered to establish and expand settlements, firm up their authority, and dominate the feared and barely understood Natives. In 1637, Plymouth and Massachusetts sought to eliminate the Pequot tribe. The Mohegans and Narragansetts allied with the English in that war (for their own, very different reasons) but then fell into a long and bitter conflict. Most of the colonies favored the Mohegans, despite suspicions of the tribe's ambitious sachem, Uncas, thereby alienating the powerful Narragansetts and on several occasions coming perilously close to a major war in the region.

These political and diplomatic conflicts were intensified by the clash between Natives and English land use. The colonists introduced domesticated pigs and cattle that rapidly increased in number, required ever-increasing amounts of pasture, and frequently damaged Native fields and dug into their food storage pits. They also came with new crops and new ways of managing the land (such as building fences and drying wetlands) that reshaped the ecology regardless of Native desires. The English also presumed that individuals owned land in perpetuity and that the men who led communities held nearly absolute authority. Both ideas were quite foreign to Natives in the region, but most settlers assumed that Indians had the same cultural standards and expected that any conflicts would be settled in the colonial courts. In all of these ways the newcomers challenged Native villages and livelihoods and forced Indian leaders to either oppose the English or embrace these changes.

Although the economic and cultural conflicts gradually increased tension in the region, Massasoit's youngest son—who was Metacom (or Metacomet) before the English gave him the name Philip in 1660—attacked the town of Swansea to start the war only after Plymouth tried to demonstrate his subjugation. Thus, King Philip's War was ultimately a war over sovereignty as well as land.[7] While the war initially seemed a local concern, it soon swept through the region and into Maine as many tribes attacked the settlers. At the same time, some Native communities tried to remain neutral, and others like the Mohegans and Christian Indians scouted and fought alongside the colonial forces; these "rogue" elements (along with hunger and disease) played a significant role in helping the English finally win the war. This would be the most widespread and devastating war between Europeans and Natives until the French and Indian War began in 1754. It also became a fundamental turning point in relations between Indians and Anglo-Americans and an archetype for many of the conflicts in North America through the late nineteenth century.

⚜ Struggles in
one
⚜ New England

BEFORE NATIVES AND EUROPEANS met in the area that became known as New England, centuries of divergent developments had given rise to the wide differences in their societies, cultures, and polities. Europeans had experienced extensive international trade and vicious warfare, particularly since the Crusades in the eleventh century; cycles of feast and famine along with terrible epidemics that to many seemed divine punishment; and an authoritarian tradition that benefited a few with wealth and power. Most of the people lived as tenants in small farming villages and owed their lords some labor and a token in exchange for the use of the land, although a growing number lived in the vibrant, growing cities—which were also death traps of disease and violence. By comparison, Native peoples lived in stable, well-established relationships with each other and the world around them.

Natives in southern New England (as elsewhere in North America) had three levels of social connections. Every individual was born into a clan, an extended family that claimed a common ancestor and governed many significant aspects of life. Villages usually contained two or more clans with up to a few hundred people and served to organize much of everyday economic and ritual life. Finally, a tribe (like the Wampanoags) connected villages and clans with a common dialect, culture, and political leadership, but lacked stable hierarchies and could be reshaped by outside influences or internal conflicts.

Native political and religious authority was spread widely: clans were headed by their eldest members; villages were led by sachems, who sought the counsel of elders and community consensus; and tribes were ruled by one or more sachems, who were advised by councils of experienced men, as well as by village and clan leaders, who in turn were guided by the need to reach community consensus. Thus, Massasoit did not rule as a monarch, although he and sachems of other coastal tribes were increasing their authority around the time the English arrived. Women as well as men could serve as sachems and provided political advice and counsel on issues important to the community. Natives believed that all living and many inert things contained spiritual power, called *manitou*, and that the supernatural could be mobilized through rituals. Some rituals could be performed by individuals, while others required a communal setting and a qualified holy man or woman, called a pawwaw.

Tribal members shared community resources, including land, while outsiders needed permission to gain access. They generally followed a seasonal economy and viewed the land that they used as part of the community's sovereign existence. The women used clamshell hoes to mound hillocks within a small area in order to raise a densely mingled crop of corn, beans, and squash that in some areas made up three-fourths of the community's diet. Women also gathered shellfish and herbs and wove household articles. Native men fished in streams and along the coast; this was a particularly important part of the Wampanoag diet, for the huge estuaries around Narragansett Bay, Mount Hope, and Buzzard's Bay were rich sources of clams, lobsters, and other fish. Native men also hunted deer and other large mammals, although this was a more important part of the diet of inland tribes. While men grew small amounts of ritual tobacco and helped clear and prepare new fields for the crops, they regarded agriculture as women's work.

While Native cultures seemed quite stable by European standards, change—albeit on a longer scale—was also part of their lives. By 1600, thousands of years of human settlement within this region had shaped three distinct socioeconomic areas. Along the coast, where the Wampanoags, Narragansetts, and Pequots were centered, clans and village clusters were beginning to fragment into nuclear households, increasing the importance of Massasoit and other tribal sachems, as rich marine sources of food and wampum, along with the corn-bean-squash agriculture and the good hunting, allowed intensive land use and year-round residence in the same place. More egalitarian tribes, such as the Nipmucs in central New England and the Eastern Wabanakis in Maine, lived in clans and small villages in the spring and fall, but for the winter they moved out into smaller hunting camps; those in southern New England farmed, while those farther north and more inland focused on fishing, hunting, and gathering. Tribes along the wide middle sections of the Connecticut River seemed to straddle the two systems, living in large villages much of the year, although men left to hunt and fish. Throughout the region, people organized their lives within the linked associations formed by clan, village, and tribe.

By comparison, European societies and political structures were more hierarchical and authoritarian, and resources flowed upward to those with power, leaving those below much poorer. This structure was echoed in the Catholic Church, with its pope, cardinals, and bishops, which also tried to monopolize and regulate knowledge. Europe also had a very strong patriarchy: men farmed and women had little power, particularly in England, where only men could own land and only the small percentage with sufficient land could participate in politics.

In the 1500s, the Renaissance and trade with Africa, Asia, and the Americas caused rapid changes that ripped the social and economic fabric. A sudden push for religious reformation in the sixteenth century, triggered by Martin Luther's protest, and the inevitable reaction by the Catholic Church added to the turmoil. Kings, noblemen, and merchants all sought power and riches, and the New World offered tremendous opportunities as well as terrors. England came late to this scramble, but after defeating the Spanish Armada in 1588, it became one of the dominant powers in Europe and sought its share of riches in eastern North America. Englishmen of all ranks believed that this "new land" could solve many of their national and personal problems; those who felt that the English Crown and its Church were headed to hell also felt that they might be able to escape God's inevitable wrath and create a righteous community on the other side of the Atlantic.

The initial meetings between Natives and Europeans in southern New England were occasional encounters between the inhabitants of coastal villages and explorers such as Giovanni da Verrazzano in 1542, Samuel Champlain in

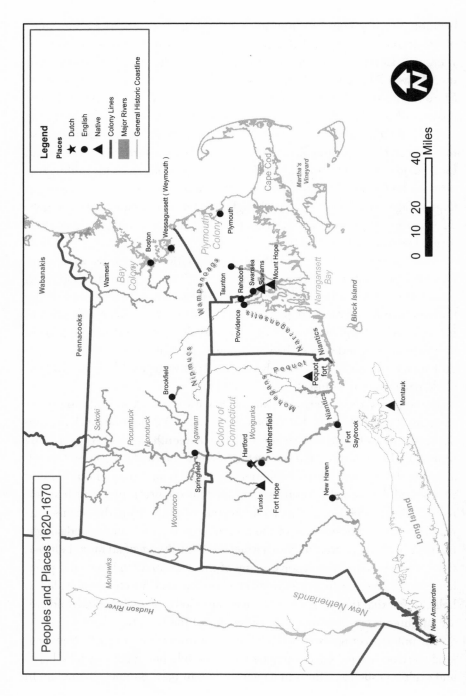

Peoples and Places, 1620–70

1604 and 1605, and John Smith from Virginia in 1616. These encounters had unforeseen but important effects on Native groups. Social and political networks were reshaped among villages and tribes in New England; some leaders were able to increase their authority, while others lost prestige or faced raids by other groups seeking resources for trade with the Europeans. More significantly, beginning in 1617, an epidemic brought by Europeans killed a huge percentage of coastal Indians from southern Maine to Narragansett Bay. Among those most affected were the Patuxets, part of the Wampanoag tribe, who lived along the bay that Smith had named Plymouth: many died, perhaps up to 90 percent, and many villages were completely decimated or abandoned by the few survivors, including the site of a Patuxet village where the first boatload of English colonists decided to settle.

These colonists, which we now call Pilgrims, were known then as Separatists, that is, they saw the Church of England as hopelessly corrupt and sought to create their own completely separate church and community—which, given the social and political norms of the period, meant that they had to flee England to avoid whippings, fines, and worse. Some came from their temporary refuge in the Netherlands, while others came directly from England. Their advance party disembarked at Nauset on Cape Cod in November 1620, but they moved across the bay to Patuxet after encountering Native hostility. The invaders renamed the village Plymouth. While the vacant village's fields were still useable, the colonists had few supplies and knew little about the area, so many died during the winter.

Wampanoags living in the neighborhood hesitated before making contact with the newcomers. When Massasoit, who lived at the other end of the tribe's territory, on the west side of Mount Hope Bay, heard of the arrival of a group of Europeans with women and children, he began discussing with his advisors the prospect of making connections with the newcomers. Their foremost concern was the rising power of the neighboring Narragansetts, who had been barely affected by the recent epidemics and were extending their influence in the region.

In the spring, the Wampanoags held a three-day gathering near Patuxet, no doubt to discuss their strategy and for preparatory rituals before meeting the English. Two Native outsiders, Samoset (a visiting Eastern Wabanaki) and Squanto (a Patuxet who had been kidnapped, taken to Spain, and then reached England before returning), were dispatched to make contact with the English. The colonists had come in families, rather than in a band of single men (as in Virginia, for example), and seemed friendly and rather helpless, so the two envoys arranged the meeting between the Pilgrims and Massasoit that established the 1621 treaty. In July, four months after that initial meeting, a delegation from Plymouth traveled to Massasoit's village to cement their alliance and scout the area.

Since the Plymouth colonists had no charter from their king, they felt the need to establish direct treaty relationships outside their connection with the Wampanoag sachem and to sign treaties with nearby villages that were nominally subject to Massasoit's authority. That need became acute in September when Corbitant, a sachem of a village north of Plymouth, rallied Native leaders alarmed at Massasoit's agreement with the colonists and created an alliance with the Narragansetts. When Squanto and Hobbamock (a Wampanoag leader who had become a trusted advisor to the Plymouth settlers) investigated, they were seized by Corbitant's warriors. Hobbamock escaped and obtained the help of the colonists. Plymouth then wrote a treaty in which a number of sachems swore allegiance to King James. A Plymouth contingent sailed a few days later for Massachusetts Bay, where they established cordial relations with Pawtucket and Massachusett villages. The English also responded to a diplomatic challenge from the Narragansett, in the form of a snakeskin, with their own defiance by returning it filled with musket shot. The English and Wampanoags finished the year with a shared harvest festival—the famous first Thanksgiving—which was traditional in both cultures.

Other English settlers soon joined the Separatists in the region. During that initial decade, fishermen and adventurers created a few additional small outposts. In 1622, London merchant Thomas Weston sent sixty men to establish the second English settlement at Wessagussett, north of Plymouth among the Massachusetts. The Wessagussett settlers proved unable to provide for themselves. While some managed to live with the Natives, others pilfered food. In anger, the local sachem Pecksuot confronted the settlers. "Some of you steal our corn," he told them, "and I have sent you word times without number & yet our corn is stolen."

When the English tried to blame one individual, beating him and offering him to Pecksuot for more punishment, the sachem rejected the sacrifice and angrily charged that "you all steal my corn."[1] Such theft was indeed common among some early settlers unable to grow or trade for food. One of them, Phineas Pratt, feared that the Indians would attack in retribution and fled for Plymouth, staggering into town after wandering in the woods all night. Massasoit had already urged the Separatists to consider a preemptive strike against a supposed uprising. Pratt's description of events seemed to confirm the plot and the need to take action. The Massachusett sachems were invited into a meeting and then killed without warning. Wessagussett was abandoned.

A Flood of Puritans

Truly significant changes came with the "Great Migration" of English Puritans to Massachusetts Bay, north of Plymouth, beginning in 1630. Their leaders felt little need to formalize relations with the Natives: they brought with them a charter from King Charles and initially had to deal with only a few scattered native villages. Puritan attitudes resulted in part from the European notion of discovery, which awarded sovereignty and territorial rights to whichever (European) nation first claimed a particular part of the Americas, and their embrace of the legal doctrine *vacuum domicilium*, which held that those who "improved" a particular area (i.e., grew crops or raised cattle on it) had the right to that land—and the colonists felt (incorrectly) that the Natives were hunters rather than farmers. As John Winthrop, the first governor of Massachusetts, put it, Indians who "inclose noe land neither have any settled habitation nor any tame cattle to improve the land" could be ethically displaced and the colonists could take land as long as "we leave them sufficient for their use."[2] At the same time, these colonists knew that it was important to create and maintain good relations with the Indians, who saw the newcomers as dangerous but potentially useful.

But as Roger Williams and a few other colonists pointed out, Wampanoags and other Natives did far more than "wander after the chase": they shaped the landscape by frequent burnings of underbrush and their slash-and-burn agriculture, which also created forest edges beloved by deer—and therefore useful for hunters. They also built huge river and tideland fish traps (weirs) that provided a rich marine diet and allowed Wampanoag villages and those of other coastal tribes to stay in place year-round. Although inland tribes tended to follow a seasonal subsistence cycle, those in southern New England did grow much of their food, and all Native groups caught or killed game in distinct, traditional territories. Hostilities could and did erupt if members of one tribe hunted, fished, or grew crops in areas held or claimed by another.

While Native landholding continued to be communal, in England landholding had been moving toward ownership in severalty, with titles vested in individuals supported by the courts—although through the 1600s many colonial villages continued to manage land and resources communally. Another difference between Natives and colonists was that the former viewed a given area in terms of its use and resources, whereas the latter saw it as a commodity; therefore, when Indians signed land deeds and treaties with the English, they often maintained the right to share one or more resources on the land, whereas the colonists expected a transfer of full possession.

There was at least one striking and very important similarity in how the Natives and the colonists in the region viewed landholding. Both peoples conceived of land as sovereign territory—a level of property distinct from ownership. While English concepts of land ownership were vague and often confusing—the differences between the commons, public lands, and lands used by households were not always distinct—their concept of sovereignty as the ultimate power over a given area was quite clear. Native concepts of sovereignty were similar, even though they viewed landholding in terms of community usufruct rather than individual ownership. This shared value would fuel King Philip's War, because it meant that both the Wampanoag sachem and Plymouth's leaders viewed their territory in terms of its political as well as economic and social significance.

The Puritan newcomers immediately played a significant diplomatic role in the region. In August 1631, Winthrop became the peacemaker between the Pennacooks and Wabanakis north of Boston in negotiating the release of the wife of a sachem who had been captured in a raid. In April 1632, Plymouth again became involved in the conflict between Massasoit and the Narragansetts. Two years later, Roger Williams, the Salem minister whose iconoclastic views alarmed many Massachusetts leaders, played a major role in negotiating a peace between the two tribes. These diplomatic encounters would become even more significant as the brewing conflict around the Thames and Connecticut rivers erupted into war between the English and the Pequots.

As more Puritans poured into the Massachusetts Bay Colony, they established new towns around Boston. Their founders focused on obtaining grants from the Massachusetts government because most believed that Native peoples lacked legal rights to the land. But various factors, including efforts by other entrepreneurs to establish settlements and the ire of English officials, led the colony's leaders to also make formal purchases from sachems. Massachusetts leaders soon became concerned that Natives angered at English expansion might attack Boston; while an eruption of smallpox in 1633 destroyed any incipient opposition, the colony continued to purchase land from sachems in order to avoid conflicts and challenges to their settlements.

In the 1630s, Native leaders elsewhere in the region offered land to colonists who seemed helpful. One important motive was the long-standing competition for access to European traders along Long Island Sound. In 1633, the sachem of the Tunxis, from about fifty miles up the Connecticut River, asked Plymouth officials to establish a trading post in his territory, providing direct access to metal tools and other European goods and an advantage over his rival Pequots. That advantage would not last long: three years later, much farther up the Connecticut River, William Pynchon obtained a deed from the Agawam sachem to establish a trading post on land that would become Springfield, for decades the western outpost of Massachusetts.

Another motive was the desire to help a friend. In 1634, the Narragansetts gave land to Roger Williams, who had developed close relations with the sachems of the tribe, just before he was driven out of the Bay Colony, in part because of his support for Native sovereignty and in part because he denied the right of civil authorities to regulate religious affairs—an idea considered dangerously heretical. Along with other dissidents and exiles from Massachusetts, Williams founded the town of Providence at the tip of Narragansett Bay. Decades later, that town established the colony of Rhode Island and Providence Plantations, along with Portsmouth on Aquidneck Island, founded by Anne Hutchison and her followers in 1638, and Shawomet (now Warwick), settled by Samuel Gorton and his company in 1643. Negotiations over land became an important part of diplomacy, particularly in the wake of the Pequot War as various groups of colonists and Indians maneuvered for survival and advantage. It would also be one of the primary causes of King Philip's War.

The Pequot War

Native groups in the region found that the growing English presence, along with other factors, required them to forge new diplomatic and trading relationships. The 1633 smallpox epidemic decimated coastal and river Indian villages but had relatively few effects on the Narragansetts and Pequots. Both tribes traded with the Dutch at Fort Hope (modern Hartford), but the Narragansetts soon dominated because their territory was a rich source of quahogs and whelks, from which wampum was made, and the Dutch wanted wampum for trade elsewhere. The Pequots tried but failed to shatter this trade alliance, and they lost their chief sachem to a Dutch raid. In desperation, Sassacus, the new Pequot sachem, offered the Bay Colony a site for a trading post along the Connecticut River if the English would arrange a truce with the Narragansetts. Massachusetts agreed, but it asked for and received tribute and title to the whole Connecticut River valley and also demanded that the tribe hand over the individuals suspected of killing the English sea captain John Stone and his crew.

The imposed agreement became one of the major steps along the road to the Pequot War, as English settlements sprouted along the Connecticut River and the Pequots began to feel besieged. Tribal leaders found their situation increasingly tenuous as they tried to meet the continued English demands to turn over Stone's murderers, compete with the Narragansetts, and maintain the allegiance of outlying villages. Sassacus began to lose power as some of his counselors, such as Wequash, began to strike out on their own and seek new alliances with the English or even join with Uncas and his Mohegans, who were closely allied with leaders of the newly established Connecticut colony and wanted Sassacus's power. In early 1636, a group of English investors built Fort Saybrook at the mouth of the Connecticut River, signaling to the Pequots and their rivals that the English intended to become a permanent power in the area.

The Pequots' precarious position emphasized how the Narragansetts had become the most powerful tribe in southern New England by 1636. They dominated the lucrative fur trade with the Dutch and established excellent relations with the English through Roger Williams. When trader John Oldham was found murdered on his ship near Block Island, the Narragansett leaders to whom the Block Islanders gave tribute and allegiance were the obvious suspects. But the Narragansetts were no longer willing to alienate the English colonists, and they saw a way to advance their own interests by promising the Bay Colony to seek revenge against the Pequots for apparently harboring those responsible for Oldham's murder. Massachusetts remained suspicious of the Narragansetts' complicity in the deed, however, and was also interested in undermining the autonomy of the dissident colony and gaining parts of Narragansett territory.

In August 1636, Massachusetts dispatched an expedition under John Endecott to obtain revenge for Oldham. After finding the Block Island villages deserted, Endecott proceeded to Connecticut to demand satisfaction from the Pequots. Negotiations went nowhere, but the colonists' raids on nearby

Pequot villages accomplished little but to inspire their warriors to raid English settlements and to kill isolated colonists in the area.

The Pequots also sought to establish an alliance with the Narragansetts against the English, arguing that "the English were strangers, and began to overspread their country, and would deprive them thereof in time, if they were suffered to grow and increase; and if the Narragansetts did assist the English to subdue them, that did but make way for their own overthrow; for if they were rooted out, the English would soon take occasion to subjugate them."[3] But in October, through the agency of Williams and the Massachusett sachem Cutshamekin, the Bay Colony persuaded Miantonomi and two sons of Canonicus to sign a treaty in which they agreed to fully support the colonists in their war against the Pequots. The Pequots continued to hit English outposts, and in February 1637 they surrounded and (unsuccessfully) tried to isolate Fort Saybrook.

As winter turned to spring, Pequot raids intensified; on April 23, they killed nine colonists in an attack on Wethersfield. Connecticut and Massachusetts mobilized ninety men and sought Plymouth's assistance. Connecticut enlisted the eager assistance offered by the Mohegan sachem Uncas, who sent seventy warriors to join the colonial force at Fort Saybrook, and Massachusetts tried to cement their unstable alliance with the Narragansetts. Ironically, given postwar antagonisms, Miantonomi was the colonists' greatest supporter in Narragansett councils. John Mason at Saybrook decided to avoid a potentially disastrous direct attack on Sassacus and instead take ship to Narragansett Bay where they could ask Miantonomi for warriors and safe conduct to attack the Pequots from the east. The Narragansett sachem was initially reluctant to take a direct role in the campaign, but two days later a band of Narragansetts caught up with the English at an eastern Niantic village and enthusiastically joined the small army.

After a long march, on May 26 this force hit the Pequot fort on the Mystic River. Their tactics of surrounding the village and attacking just as the sun began to rise, along with their decision to burn the village when they encountered resistance, resulted in the death of nearly all of its four to six hundred inhabitants. These were mostly women and children, since Sassacus and his main body of warriors had gone to another village, Weinshauks. The English tactics and massacre of the Pequots horrified their Native allies, who "much rejoiced at our victories, and greatly admired the manner of *English* mens fight: but cried *mach it, mach it*; that is, it is naught, it is naught, because it is too furious, and slays too many men."[4] Many Narragansetts left, leaving the Puritan-Indian force greatly weakened and vulnerable, particularly when about three hundred Pequots came upon their rear as they began retreating toward the Thames River. A brief firefight and the shock of the Mystic attack kept the Pequots at a distance. Word of the staggering Pequot defeat spread quickly, and three days later the Montauk leader Wyandanch crossed from Long Island to Fort Saybrook to ensure good relations with the English colonists.

The Pequots at Weinshauks were shocked and horrified by their defeat. They held a meeting to discuss whether to attack the Narragansetts, attack the English, or seek safety to the west. Sassacus "was all for bloud," but most warriors urged flight.[5] Some went to Long Island or Block Island or sought refuge with the Narragansetts rather than face the English or Mohegans. The largest group, with about three hundred men led by Sassacus, headed west, hoping to join the Mohawks, but they were closely followed by Mohegan bands and soon by a fresh colonial force. On July 14, another major battle at a swamp west of Quinnipac (later New Haven) resulted in the capture of 180 Pequots and the killing of many more. Sassacus escaped with his brother and other Pequot sachems and finally reached Mohawk country. But there in early August he and his party were set upon and slaughtered by those who he had hoped would provide refuge.

The English destruction of the Pequots reshaped relationships between different Native communities, scrambling tribal alliances and boundaries along both sides of Long Island Sound. The Mohegans displaced the Pequots as the leading Native group along the Thames River, and Uncas used his loyalty to the English as leverage to increase his power throughout Connecticut and beyond. The Niantic sachem Ninigret, who had remained neutral in the war but had kinship relations with the Pequots and Narragansetts, gained new influence among the Narragansetts and prominence with the English. The English were clearly the greatest beneficiaries: they destroyed a major barrier to their expansion into Connecticut and eastern Long Island, gained a reputation for belligerence, and became the greatest power in New England.

Conflicts between Mohegans and Narragansetts

Tensions immediately emerged between the victors. On August 20, Roger Williams met with Canonicus and Miantonomi to warn the two Narragansett sachems that Massachusetts leaders feared they were seeking to become the greatest power in the region by monopolizing Pequot wampum and warriors and asserting their authority over villages that had been Pequot allies. The two denied the accusation, listed their own complaints against the colony, and warned Governor Winthrop through Williams that Uncas and his Mohegans were the false ones.[6] The disagreements between the Narragansetts and Massachusetts were seemingly resolved when Miantonomi came to Boston on November 9. The sachem reaffirmed his recognition of Massachusetts rights to Pequot territory and Block Island, and the colonists agreed to recognize his authority over Ninigret and some of the surviving Pequot sachems.

But throughout the following year, conflict roiled between the Mohegans and Narragansetts over the spoils of the war. In late February 1638, Williams again met with the Narragansetts to tell them that Connecticut wanted to meet. The tribe's sachems told Williams that the Connecticut men were untrustworthy and that the Mohegans were secretly "adopting" Pequot remnants rather than treating them as war captives, and they asked the colonists to ensure that captives would be shared as per previous agreements. When Uncas traveled to Boston in May—probably to reassure the colonists of his loyalty—Bay Colony authorities demanded that he allow them to decide the fate of Pequot captives and that he work to settle his conflict with the Narragansetts. Uncas then swore allegiance to all of the English colonies.

Ninigret and his Eastern Niantics, closely connected to the Narragansetts, were also involved in the postwar turmoil. Late in July, Ninigret crossed to Long Island and tried to strong-arm a Montauk village allied with Connecticut into becoming his tributaries. Montauk sachem Wyandanch complained to his English allies, who notified Massachusetts; Winthrop in turn passed word to Roger Williams, who told Miantonomi that the colony would go to war against the Niantics if they did not make restitution. Ninigret checked with Williams, who assured him that the colonists were serious. The Niantic sachem then hastily met with Connecticut representatives and agreed to repay all of the wampum taken from the Montauks.

In August, Connecticut demanded that Miantonomi come to Hartford to answer charges that he was hiding Pequot captives and to sign a treaty that superseded the treaty signed before the war with Massachusetts. The colony also summoned Uncas and the Mohegans. Connecticut had two goals: to ensure its security by dampening the conflict between Uncas and Miantonomi, and to reduce the influence of Massachusetts Bay. The Narragansett agreed to the conference, to be held in mid-September, but carefully brought Williams to avoid diplomatic entrapment and other sachems and warriors to avoid a Mohegan ambush—a useful precaution, since some of their allies headed to the conference were robbed by Mohegan warriors. In Hartford, there were public shows of friendship and private meetings that revealed deep suspicions and hostility. The resulting treaty required Narragansett and Mohegan leaders to submit all future complaints to the English, gave each tribe an equal number of Pequots and required that a tax be paid for each Pequot they held, claimed Pequot territory for the English, and declared that tribe extinct.

But the Pequots did not remain extinct for very long. In 1638, Roger Williams reported five small groups along the Thames River, in addition to those living with Uncas or Ninigret, on Long Island, and elsewhere. Within five years, the English (particularly Connecticut) found it useful to officially recognize the reconstitution of two clearly subordinate Pequot groups, largely to counter the potential threat of an overly ambitious Uncas. The two would over the next few decades become known as the Stonington Pequots and Mashantucket Pequots. Uncas and Mohegan warriors continued to try to force these communities to become part of his tribe; when the Pequots and their English neighbors complained, the United Colonies—an organization created by Massachusetts, Connecticut, Plymouth, and New Haven to coordinate policy—rebuked the sachem and provided reservations for the two Pequot tribes. In September 1654, the United Colonies declared all Pequot remnants under their protection, and a few years later they gave those groups access to wampum shell beds on Long Island. When King Philip's War broke out, the Pequots repaid this support with their loyalty and their warriors.

Despite this apparent settlement, the English colonists continued to pressure the Narragansetts. A cow owned by a Salem man was found killed, and Massachusetts authorities demanded that the tribe pay an exorbitant fine of £100. The Narragansetts protested that the responsible individuals should be asked for restitution, just as the English did, and that no one within their tribe had committed the deed, but the colonists found it impossible to identify and gain satisfaction from individual Natives and therefore held sachems responsible. The Puritans also believed that the tribe was violating the treaty by taking too many Pequot captives and tolerating attacks of those Pequots against English fishermen. Connecticut took action to keep Pequot territory for that colony, sending in 1639 a large force under John Mason and Uncas to evict Niantics and Narragansetts attempting to settle there. This incident and efforts by the English to deny hunting rights to the Narragansetts in the "conquered" territory increased the tribe's growing resentment.

Cold War with the Narragansetts

Between the end of the Pequot War and the shattering cataclysm of King Philip's War, the Narragansetts experienced an extended cold war with Massachusetts and Connecticut. The decades of tension were frequently punctuated by moments of conflict that threatened wider war, particularly when Uncas manipulated his English connections, Ninigret tried to gain power, or the colonists tried to chop away at the tribe's allies and lands. The Narragansetts pinned most of the blame for their troubles on Uncas, and they became openly angry at the English only when the colonists abused them or showed obvious favoritism toward the Mohegans. The many-sided, complex conflict formed the diplomatic and political landscape of southern New England at midcentury and, to a significant degree, shaped the responses of the colonists, Narragansetts, and Mohegans to the outbreak of war in 1675.

By the summer of 1640, the colonists believed that Miantonomi was forging a hostile alliance with the Mohawks—the feared Iroquois tribe whose warriors raided hundreds of miles from home. Massachusetts sent a delegation to the Narragansetts seeking reassurance. Miantonomi and his councilors agreed to everything, but Ninigret (who was also present) refused to appear agreeable and insisted on being recognized as an equal to the English king. The Niantic sachem would take an increasingly active role in Narragansett politics, and he rejected the tribe's agreement to yield important Pequot refugees to the Bay Colony. As a result, the colonists began to fear Ninigret as well as Miantonomi. Roger Williams reassured John Winthrop that the Narragansetts had the best intentions, but that fugitive Pequots were being hidden by Uncas among his Mohegans. In November 1640, Miantonomi traveled to Boston. Bay Colony leaders tried again to use the offensive Pequot interpreter, and when Miantonomi objected, Governor Winthrop violated diplomatic protocol by refusing to host the visiting sachem. As a result, the two reached no agreement, and Miantonomi left angry.

Tensions between the English and the Narragansetts increased in the aftermath of the Boston meeting. The Narragansetts were angered at the support Connecticut gave to Uncas and his Mohegans, at the demands by Massachusetts and Connecticut for large amounts of tribute (which not only was difficult to fulfill but showed a clear desire to dominate trade and politics), and by the effects of the spreading colonial settlements. In 1642, Miantonomi made several trips to the Montauks to plead for an alliance against the colonial threat, although the sachem's primary goal may have been to shore up his position against the Mohegans. However, the Montauks refused to oppose the English.

On the English side, fears and rumors were widespread. In August 1642, Massachusetts received several letters from Connecticut cautioning that Indian allies had warned of a hostile Native alliance and urging a preemptive strike against the Narragansetts. Bay Colony leaders were loath to go to war and suspected that the admonitions originated from Uncas to manipulate the English against Miantonomi. Winthrop took the precaution of bringing the Massachusett and Pennacook sachems to Boston in order to disarm their warriors, and he summoned Miantonomi to answer charges of violating past agreements. At the conference, the Narragansett sachem insisted on confronting Uncas, who he believed was the source of the rumors. Bay Colony leaders were clearly impressed by the sachem, and in the wake of the conference they told their Connecticut counterparts to abandon any plans to strike at the Narragansetts.

While Massachusetts curbed any immediate military action, the colony increased its diplomatic efforts against neighboring dissidents allied with the Narragansetts. Samuel Gorton, leader of a group of radicals disliked by most Puritans, had obtained a deed for a new settlement along Narragansett Bay. In response, on April 22, Massachusetts persuaded Pumham and Saconoco, the sachems within whose territory Gorton's claim lay and who had been Narragansett allies, to recognize the sovereignty of the Bay Colony. This opened the door for Massachusetts to arrest Gorton and his supporters and demonstrated the colony's ability to undermine Narragansett power. Roger Williams hurried to England to obtain a charter for the now-threatened colony of Rhode Island and to seek royal support for their Narragansett allies. In response, Massachusetts, Connecticut, and New Haven joined, on May 19, 1643, in a "firm and perpetual League of Friendship and Amity for offense and defense." Plymouth ratified the agreement in August, creating the United Colonies. Rhode Island was not invited.[7]

The tensions between the Narragansetts and the United Colonies became an open conflict as that tribe clashed with Uncas. In July 1643, the Mohegan sachem complained to Connecticut that he had been attacked by Wongunks;

the colony tried to intervene, was rebuffed by that tribe's sachem, Sequasson, and gave the Mohegans permission to attack Sequasson's village. Miantonomi, committed to protecting the Wongunks but bound by treaty with Massachusetts, first obtained the Bay Colony's permission to strike Uncas. However, the Mohegans shattered the Narragansett war party, took Miantonomi prisoner, and brought him to Boston. The very first action by the United Colonies was to authorize Uncas to execute the sachem, as well as to promise the Mohegans that they would send soldiers to protect them from Narragansett revenge. Their proclamation condemned the Narragansett sachem for "his treacherous plotts" against all English in the region, including recruiting the feared Mohawks.[8]

The Narragansetts could have blamed the English for Miantonomi's execution; instead, they assailed the Mohegans and maneuvered to cement their sovereignty. In 1643 and 1644, his brother and successor Pessicus (ca. 1623–76) asked the United Colonies for permission to attack Uncas; they refused and threatened war, in part because they suspected a plot with the Mohawks. The Narragansetts responded by treating a Massachusetts delegation rudely and raiding the Mohegans, killing eleven. In April 1644, with Samuel Gorton's advice and assistance, the tribe made a formal *"voluntary and free submission"* to King Charles II in an effort to gain leverage against the United Colonies and to challenge the right of Massachusetts to claim territory. Pessicus and Canonicus declared that they could not *"yield over ourselves unto any that are subjects themselves in any case*; having ourselves been the chief sachems, or princes successfully, and of the country, time out of mind."[9]

In response, the United Colonies called Pessicus to Boston, but he refused, telling the English that "wee have subjected ourselves, our lands, and our possessions" to King Charles, so the colony should submit any issues to the king to decide between the two equally sovereign governments.[10] This was hardly reassuring to the Puritans, and, not surprisingly, the United Colonies announced that they would assist the Mohegans if that tribe was again attacked. In February 1645, Pessicus sent messengers to Boston to demand 160 fathoms of wampum in tribute from Uncas. When he received nothing, a large Narragansett force attacked the Mohegans; the day-long battle resulted in heavy losses for both tribes, although the Narragansetts retreated. In July, the United Colonies summoned the hostile parties to a conference while preparing to attack the Narragansetts. The English called off the attack after the tribe's leaders suddenly appeared, but the commissioners refused to hear complaints against Uncas and demanded hostages, two thousand fathoms of wampum, reparations for the Mohegans, and the surrender of all rights to Pequot territory. Pessicus and the others signed under duress, realizing that the alternative was a disastrous war.

The Boston conference settled nothing. In June 1646, the United Colonies accused the Narragansetts and Niantics of breaking the treaty by sending insufficient wampum. These messages received no response, although Pessicus and Ninigret both told contacts that the other sachem was responsible for paying that tribute. In September, the commissioners formally notified the tribes that they had broken the treaty and were still suspected of plotting with the Mohawks. A year later, the United Colonies again sent word that the two had violated the treaty and were suspected of planning hostilities; the English demanded a meeting. Pessicus found a polite way of sending delegates instead; Ninigret went to the conference and agreed to stay while messengers went to get the overdue tribute. They returned two weeks later with two hundred fathoms of wampum, half from each tribe. Ninigret promised to gather more if he could return home. The commissioners agreed but threatened war if a thousand fathoms more did not arrive within twenty days. As before, that deadline slipped without retribution, as all sides wished to avoid war.

The conflict between the Narragansetts and Uncas soon again involved Connecticut River Indians. The United Colonies received word that Sequasson planned to assassinate several Connecticut leaders in retaliation for their support of the judicial murder of Miantonomi. The Wongunk sachem fled to a Pocumtuck village, but Uncas attacked the village and captured Sequasson. In the aftermath of this incident, other River Indians showed their anger and contempt by burning property in Windsor and confronting delegates from the United Colonies, but having made their point, they softened their hostility with a gift of wampum. Sequasson was put on trial but was (amazingly) acquitted, and this ended his enmity against the English. Uncas continued to warn that the Pocumtucks and Wongunks were up to no good, but few colonists believed him, particularly after other Indian groups such as the Nipmucs lodged complaints against his warriors.

Still, the English continued to be concerned that Indians were conspiring against the colonies. That same summer, for example, the Narragansett sachems sent a gift of wampum to a visiting delegation of Mohawks, leading to rumors that the tribes were plotting war. The United Colonies dispatched a delegation to collect overdue tribute and to demand information about this possible Mohawk alliance. By that time, Canonicus, who for decades had shared leadership of the tribe with Miantonomi, had died and been succeeded by his eldest son Mixanno (?–ca. 1657). After making the English delegates wait, Mixanno joined Pessicus in their meeting at the home of Roger Williams. The sachems told the colonists that the wampum was an annual gift to the Mohawks and reassured the colonists that they intended to pay the fine.

The fears of the United Colonies were magnified by the way in which the Narragansetts and Rhode Island's leadership supported each other. On May 28, 1650, they signed a treaty (which unfortunately no longer exists). Three months later, the United Colonies finally took action, sending a delegation to demand the outstanding 308 fathoms of wampum from the Narragansetts and authorizing Massachusetts to begin war preparations. Delegation head Captain Humphrey Atherton persuaded Roger Williams to act as their interpreter and initially seemed to reach an accommodation with the tribe. But as the Narragansetts were conferring in Pessicus's wigwam, Atherton suddenly entered, dragged Pessicus out by his hair, and threatened to take both Pessicus and Ninigret by force. Williams persuaded the soldiers to wait at his house for the wampum and paid them ten fathoms to keep the peace. Ninigret and the Narragansetts brought enough to have the "debt" cancelled and avoid war, and Williams wrote a bitter letter to Connecticut governor John Winthrop Jr., condemning the United Colonies' "Partialitie" toward Uncas.[11]

Widening Conflict

This quarrel soon expanded to involve the Montauks of eastern Long Island and the Dutch of New Netherlands. In December 1647, New Haven's governor warned Massachusetts that a Dutch agent in Saybrook had told Indians that his nation was about to war with the English and had "ingaged" many of the Natives as allies.[12] Five years later, England declared war on the Netherlands over trade issues. Puritans feared that Dutch merchants were selling guns to Indians, and Uncas along with Native leaders on Long Island told Connecticut that the Dutch were trying to recruit Narragansetts and Niantics against the English. In April, the United Colonies sent very pointed questions to Ninigret, Pessicus, and Mixanno asking about the charges that they were conspiring with the Mohawks and the Dutch. All three denied the charges, although Ninigret admitted that he had visited New Amsterdam to see a doctor. But Puritan fears remained, fed by reports that the Dutch were

Metacom, a.k.a. King Philip. This is the earliest known drawing of Metacom, although there is no evidence that it was based on descriptions of the sachem, and except for the wampum belt the clothing and weapons seem to echo mid-eighteenth-century Ohio Valley tribes rather than the Wampanoags in the late seventeenth century. Engraving by Paul Revere in Thomas Church, *The Entertaining History of King Philip's War* (1716; Newport, RI: Solomon Southwick, 1772). Courtesy Library of Congress.

urging Natives to burn English homes and then shoot the inhabitants. Connecticut and New Haven began preparations to strike at New Netherlands, but Massachusetts refused to participate, thus preventing war.

Ninigret may have been working with the Dutch to overthrow Wyandanch and become sachem of the Montauks. At some point, he came to Massachusetts governor John Endecott, accused Wyandanch of killing his men, and asked permission to seek revenge. According to Roger Williams, Endecott gave implicit approval. In the late spring of 1653, Ninigret's men attacked Wyandanch's village, killing at least thirty and taking fourteen prisoners, including the Montauk sachem's daughter. Although representatives from several colonies urged sending troops to attack Ninigret, Massachusetts's commissioner vetoed the action, calling the conflict between Ninigret and Wyandanch not within their jurisdiction. Uncas saw an opening and offered to attack Ninigret for a price.

As Uncas became involved, the Niantic-Montauk conflict became part of the long-standing enmity between the Mohegans and the Narragansetts, even drawing in the Pocumtucks and reviving the threat of Mohawk attacks. The United Colonies saw this widening war as a great threat, particularly since there were now English settlements on Long Island, and in September 1654 told Ninigret to stop raiding the Montauks and demanded that he and Uncas come to Hartford to reach a settlement. But the Montauks had attacked a group of Niantics visiting Block Island, adding the motive of revenge to Ninigret's ambition. Rumors again began circulating that Ninigret was plotting with the Dutch.

On their side, Ninigret and the Narragansetts heard rumors of English threats to attack if the Indians did not become Christians, and they asked Roger Williams to intervene with Parliament "that they might not be forced from their Religion."[13] On October 5, the United Colonies decided to declare war on Ninigret and sent a force of sixty men to pressure the sachem. Ninigret finally agreed to speak with two delegates, and on October 18 he signed a treaty to pay long-promised tribute and surrender his remaining Pequots. But tensions remained: in February 1655, John Garriard of Warwick robbed the grave of Pessicus's sister, nearly triggering an attack against the town.

In September 1656, the conflict between Uncas and the Narragansetts flared again. Mixanno went to a United Colonies meeting to charge the Mohegan sachem with "abusively naming and Jeering his dead Ancestors" and challenged the sachem to battle. A new war was avoided as the English promised to look into the charges, told the Narragansetts not to attack Uncas, and rebuked the Mohegan for provoking the tribe.[14] But the Narragansetts continued to pursue their long-standing vendetta. In July 1657, for example, probably to intimidate the colonists, they warned Connecticut authorities that large numbers of Mohawks were coming to attack Uncas, and that the English settlers would be harmed if they got in the way. The English took the threat seriously and again warned the Narragansetts not to take part.

At the end of the decade, Narragansett leadership had become much weaker. Pessicus was not as strong or respected as Miantonomi. When Mixanno died, his authority was claimed by his widow Quaiapen, his cousin, and his two sons. This relative void allowed Ninigret to increase his influence within the tribe to the point where he was often perceived as its chief sachem. The situation also emboldened Uncas to raid Nipmuc and Narragansett communities along the edges of Mohegan territory, including Cowesett, Quinnapaug, and Quabaug. The situation was further confused when the Wampanoag sachem, Wamsutta, told the United Colonies that the Quabaugs were his subjects and that he had recently fought Uncas for authority over the village.[15]

The Narragansett-Mohegan conflict again spilled over into the Connecticut River valley in May 1658, after a young man killed a relative of Sequasson and fled to Pocumtuck. Sequasson asked his former enemy Uncas to help him obtain justice, and despite an effort by Connecticut to mediate, he insisted on blood vengeance. For the next few years the Pocumtucks and other Wabanakis, joined by Tunxis and Narragansett warriors, continued to attack the Mohegans, occasionally frightening colonial settlers in the area. In mid-September 1658, the Pocumtucks attacked a party of Mohegans and Englishmen headed for peace negotiations and then raided Wethersfield for corn. The United Colonies seemed more puzzled than angry and asked the Pocumtucks to explain their actions. At a conference a year later, the Pocumtucks told the English that they could not negotiate a treaty with the Mohegans without the approval of their allies. Tensions escalated when Pocumtuck warriors attacked Jonathan Brewster's trading post, which was on Mohegan territory, because Brewster had provided Uncas with weapons and was sheltering twenty Mohegans.

The result was the infamous Atherton Deed of 1660, which added to the long list of Narragansett grievances against the English. The United Colonies decided that this tribe was the real culprit in the Pocumtuck-Mohegan conflict and fined them the huge sum of 595 fathoms of wampum. On September 29, 1660, three Narragansett sachems agreed to pay the fine within four months; if they did not, they would lose their remaining lands, about four hundred square miles. Two years earlier, a group of prominent Puritans from several colonies had established the Narragansett Proprietors, better known as the Atherton Company, to speculate in Narragansett lands and undercut Rhode Island and Narragansett authority. The proprietors agreed to pay the fine in exchange for a mortgage on the tribal lands. But the tribe was unable to pay the mortgage, and the proprietors claimed their prize in 1662. A tidal wave of legal controversies followed, endangering the Narragansetts and Rhode Island. In an effort to regain their lands, the tribe sought and obtained formal recognition of their sovereignty in November 1663 from the newly restored King Charles II. A year later, a visiting royal commission rejected the Atherton Deed as fraudulent but failed to stop the claim.

Struggles over Land

In mid-1642, just five years after the Pequot War, the Narragansett sachem Miantonomi went with his counselors to the Montauks on eastern Long Island to forge an alliance against the increasingly numerous and powerful colonists, who were creating many new settlements with growing herds of cattle. In one of the most famous Native speeches from this period, the Narragansett sachem told the Montauks that "we [must] be one as they are, otherwise we shall be gone shortly, for you know our fathers had plenty of deer and skins, our plains were full of deer, as also our woods, and of turkies, and our coves full of fish and fowl. But these English having gotten our land, they with scythes cut down the grass, and with axes fell the trees; their cows and horses eat the grass, and their hogs spoil our clam banks, and we shall all be starved."[16]

In the wake of the Pequot War, conflicts between Natives and settlers over land and resources escalated throughout southern New England, driven by deep differences between how Natives and colonists used land. Compared with their Native neighbors, New England villages began to look more like market societies with the sprouting seeds of capitalism already present. Merchants were eager to buy New England timber, beaver pelts, and fish, and so those resources were quickly valued not for their immediate utility but for the price they would bring in the international market. The colonists felled forests for fuel, shelter, export, and simply to clear land for farming and pasture, altering the watershed and drying or flooding large areas. Plants and animals brought by the settlers pushed out native flora and fauna. The European's quest for beaver pelts drove that animal nearly to extinction in New England, causing many ponds to become meadows and other kinds of ecological changes. Natives were involved in these transformations: even before English colonization they trapped beaver to trade to the Dutch and the French, and as settlements came close to Indian villages, Native men sometimes worked for Anglo-American farmers or sold them fish, deer meat, and other products.

But the greatest cause of conflict came with English cattle and pigs, for Natives had domesticated only the dog. Cattle required much more land for pasture than was needed for food crops, multiplying the colonists' seemingly constant demand for more territory. The English enclosed their crops rather than their pastures, allowing wandering cattle to find food and water more easily and breed faster. They insisted that the Indians do the same, but the Indians had never constructed fences and thought that the English should instead erect barriers around their animals. Colonists refused, resulting in wandering cattle that ate Indian corn and consumed wild food needed by the deer hunted by Natives. When Metacom listed his grievances just before the outbreak of war, one was that "the English Catell and horses still increased," to the point that "when [the Indians] removed 30 mill [miles] from wher the English had anything to do, they Could not kepe ther coren from being spoyled, they never being used to fence, and thoft [thought] when the English boft [bought] land of them that thay woud hav kept their Catell upone their owne land."[17]

The colonists also let their pigs go wild, leading to feral swine digging into Indian storage pits to consume the dried food they had stashed for the winter and devouring the clams that formed an important part of the Native diet. But when an Indian killed a trespassing cow or pig, the English owner would have the local constable arrest the outraged "culprit," generating broader conflicts. Although after midcentury the colonies did begin to pass laws that attempted to provide special avenues of appeal to Natives, or the right to seize cattle and hold them until the owner paid damages, these measures were never properly enforced or effective.

Native peoples in the region tried to adapt in various ways, living in larger and more permanent settlements, taking on English clothing and housing as local materials became scarcer, going to justices of the peace with their complaints about English violations, or having their sachems meet in conference with the colonial leaders. Some took on animal husbandry, which in European culture served as the ultimate symbol of domestication and civilized landholding. While the Christian Indians were particularly famous for this adaptation, in the 1660s even Metacom began raising pigs. Although Natives initially hated the pestiferous swine, calling them "cut-throats," pig raising was not as radical a change in aboriginal culture as might appear at first. Pigs were apt substitutes for the increasingly scarce deer: they needed little care, and when allowed to go feral, they fit within traditional gender roles distinguishing men (hunting) from women (agriculture). But ironically, Metacom's adoption of this civilized husbandry angered Plymouth because the sachem was able to sell his pork for less than the colony's farmers.

These substantive changes in land uses and economic habits meant that Native villages adjoining the English settlements and farms were increasingly forced to observe the colonists' property laws and to go to the colonial courts to get conflicts with the settlers resolved. The colonists viewed sachems incorrectly as similar to their own magistrates and held them responsible for any illegal actions by their people, even though their primary duty was to provide or organize information and resources for the community. English expectations therefore reinforced colonial domination.

Many colonists also proved skilled at manipulating their laws as well as finding illicit means to take land from the Indians. Englishmen plied Natives with liquor and then persuaded them to sign deeds that they could not read. They bought areas from people who did not live there, or who lacked the authority to part with community resources or rights. They charged individuals with petty crimes or debt, usually won the judgment because the defendants rarely spoke English (and often failed to appear), and then claimed land as payment for fines or debts. In addition, the rapid decline of the fur trade after 1650 meant that Natives with debts to the colonists or whose people needed manufactured goods could meet those obligations only with land. Those who fell into this trap were often sachems. Between 1649 and 1660, for example, Massasoit sold large areas around Bridgewater, Dartmouth, and Woodcock's garrison (later Attleborough) in exchange for clothing and other goods. In 1672, Metacom himself sold twelve square miles to Taunton for £143, perhaps in part to pay the £100 fine Plymouth forced on him in the September 1671 treaty.

By the mid-seventeenth century, these issues were facing Indians living far west of Boston, along the midsection of the Connecticut River (within Massachusetts) where the colonists had established a handful of flourishing settlements. The five interrelated communities of "River Indians"—Woronoco, Agawam, Nonotuck, Pocumtuck, and Sokoki—were linked to the Nipmucs by kinship and to the Wabanaki tribes farther north by language and culture. The valley was separated from the rest of Massachusetts by rugged hills, but it featured easy routes to the interior fur trade, excellent farm land, and ready access to the ocean. Beginning in the 1630s, River Indian sachems allowed William Pynchon and his son John to obtain land for trading posts and towns, although the Natives carefully maintained their rights to hunting and fishing and continued to raise crops near the expanding colonial settlements. But by the 1660s, the English population in the valley was, as elsewhere in the region, generating growing tensions and conflicts with Natives over land, resources, and sovereignty.

The Connecticut River valley narrows as it climbs toward Canada. Slightly more than a century later, it would become the dividing line between the states of New Hampshire and Vermont. But in the mid-seventeenth century it was a pathway for the Wabanakis living north of Massachusetts. Two distinct groupings lived in this region. The tribes of Western Wabanakis in the area that became New Hampshire and Vermont were closely related to the River Indians, and the tribes of Eastern Wabanakis in Maine were generally named for the rivers and streams along which they lived. When war threatened, families and villages moved to safety, returning months or years later, or even finding new homes elsewhere. Political leadership was extremely localized, and any particular sachem generally spoke only for his clan or village.

From the Connecticut River to the Atlantic Ocean, the growing tensions over land and other resources after the Pequot War became problematic and exacerbated the tensions that led to King Philip's War. By the early 1640s, there were four English colonies with about twenty thousand settlers. By midcentury, Massachusetts and Connecticut were clearly the dominant powers in the region, and they established new villages and trading posts in the interior, generating more conflicts with Native communities over differences in ownership and land uses; Massachusetts settlers also created outposts along the southern coast of Maine, sometimes trespassing on Native fishing sites.

This movement also increasingly created new problems between Indian communities. The uncertain or contested nature of Native land ownership sometimes resulted in overlapping rights claimed by different sachems. Competition between colonies, communities, and individuals could also cause conflicts as sachems connected with particular colonies or patrons accused each other of fraud for selling land they did not own. As good land became scarcer by the middle of the century, colonists seeking advantages sometimes sought to use Indian titles to secure their claims against others. Indian leaders also sought to gain political or economic advantages by manipulating the ambitions, jealousies, and quarrels of the colonists.

These dealings over land were not just about who held, worked, and benefited from the land; conflicts over political power and sovereignty were deeply embedded in the land transactions as well as the treaties. The colonists clearly believed that land deeds or treaties recognizing colonial authority conveyed sovereignty as well as ultimate tenure to them. But the sachems putting their marks to such an agreement seem to have perceived the resulting relationship with the colony as an alliance that did not surrender sovereignty, one that allowed the colonists to use certain resources rather than granting full authority over all of the people living within the given territory. Of course, fraud was a constant threat, particularly since only a few Natives could read English and understand the colonial legal system. Metacom complained just before the war began that the English had managed to take "many miles square of land," and that when he or another sachem did sell land the purchaser or his colony would claim a larger area and then insist that only a deed could serve as evidence.[18]

Edward Randolph, sent by King James II in 1685 to investigate the colonies' obedience to royal laws, listed several possible reasons for King Philip's War. Some observers, he noted, "impute the cause to some injuries offered to the Sachim Philip; for he being possessed of a tract of land called Mount Hope, a very fertile, pleasant and rich soyle, some English had a mind to dispossess him thereof, who never wanting one pretence or other to attain their end, complained of injuries done by Philip and his Indians to their stock and cattle, whereupon Philip was often summoned before the magistrate, sometimes imprisoned, and never released but upon parting with a considerable part of his land."[19] The resulting conflict intensified when Plymouth challenged the sovereignty of the sachem and the loyalty of his people.

⚓ King Philip and
two
⚓ Plymouth

ON SEPTEMBER 13, 1671, Plymouth governor Thomas Prence and his council of war assembled to discuss what to do about the continued threat posed by Metacom, who had become the Wampanoag sachem a decade earlier. In 1662, the colony had compelled Metacom to agree not to sell land to others, and five years later Plymouth colonists established the town of Swansea near the sachem's "capitol" without obtaining the sachem's agreement; this so angered Metacom that in June he and his warriors walked through the village brandishing their muskets. Since then, rumors had swirled that Metacom was negotiating with neighboring tribes and the King's agents against Plymouth. In March 1671, the colony's council demanded that he and other Wampanoags appear to answer a colonist's charges against one of his people; he refused and his warriors threatened the messenger. One month later, as the rumors began to name the Narragansetts as Metacom's allies, Plymouth managed to get Metacom to come to Taunton for a meeting; once there, the isolated sachem was compelled to confess that he had violated the 1662 agreement and to agree to surrender his people's firearms. But soon afterward, word came that a large group of warriors were gathering at Mount Hope, with at least sixty bearing muskets.

Judging from subsequent events, Metacom was indeed forging an alliance against Plymouth. The colony's war council sent James Brown and John Walker to summon the sachem. They found him at a dance; when Brown attempted to speak with Metacom, the sachem knocked the hat off his head—an act that the colonist viewed as rude and aggressive, but which Metacom probably claimed as his due deference; after all, English rulers were recognized in that fashion. When Brown returned the next day, Metacom told him that he had already been invited by the Reverend John Eliot to come to Boston. A week later, the Wampanoag sachem met there with the Bay Colony's leaders to complain about Plymouth's violations of his sovereignty. Massachusetts offered to mediate, sending word to the smaller and weaker colony that they doubted whether Metacom "had subjected himselfe and people and country . . . any further then as in a neighborly and friendly" fashion. Plymouth's council had little choice but to accept.[1]

On Thursday, September 24, some of the most powerful men from Massachusetts, Connecticut, and Plymouth met Metacom and his counselors in the town that had once been the Wampanoag village of Patuxet. At some point, Plymouth's leaders persuaded the others that Metacom had in previous agreements with the colony surrendered his sovereignty and had since been in violation of those treaties and "carried insolently and proudly towards us on several occasions." The colonists closed ranks, and Metacom unexpectedly found himself without support. Five days later, he and five counselors reluctantly signed a treaty that began with subjugation to "the King of England, etc., and the government of Plymouth, and to their laws." The sachem promised to pay Plymouth £100 "in such things as I have," which by 1671 meant land rather than wampum or furs.[2] He also promised that he would go to Plymouth's governor with any conflicts between his people and the English, before warring with other tribes, and before selling any of his land. The colonists intended the agreement to legally subject the Wampanoags to Plymouth—to prevent them from becoming allies of Rhode Island or appealing to the king, and to allow the colony to control all of the territory between Buzzard's Bay and the Massachusetts border. It also set the stage for the war four years later.

Emerging Conflicts

Metacom's father Massasoit had, after his groundbreaking 1621 treaty, become more deeply connected to the English. The colonists twice in the early 1630s helped the Wampanoag sachem negotiate truces with the more powerful Narragansett tribe. At the eruption of the war against the Pequots, he and his tribe had become allies of the Mohegans, and so Massasoit became concerned when the English seemed to listen to Narragansett stories about Mohegan perfidy. On April 21, 1638, two weeks before his more distant ally Uncas traveled to Boston, Massasoit went to the Massachusetts capital and met with Governor John Winthrop, giving beaver skins and getting reassurance of peace.

Those connections worked. In 1646, Roger Williams went to Massasoit to obtain a deed for an area north of Providence; while he had already gained a grant to the area from the Narragansetts, the Wampanoags also claimed the area and needed to be satisfied. By 1652, English hostility to the Narragansetts had caused the leaders of some villages along the edges of tribal territory to join with Massasoit. Questions of sovereignty and conflicts over what their diplomatic and political connections meant could be avoided or ignored as long as Massasoit lived and the colonial leaders focused on managing the more immediate issues with the Narragansetts and Mohegans. But after Massasoit died, these issues evolved into the war that engulfed the entire region.

The death of the Wampanoag sachem around 1660 marked a noticeable deterioration in the tribe's relations with Plymouth. Part of the reason was the rise of new leaders in the colony, following William Bradford's death in 1657, who lacked the personal connections that the founders had held with the Natives. This second generation was far more willing to assert sovereignty and to assign land to their people without first negotiating with Wampanoag leaders. Furthermore, they had to deal with a new sachem, Wamsutta, Massasoit's older son. We know little about Wamsutta's leadership or personality, but we do know that one of his first documented actions as sachem was, in June 1660, to ask Plymouth for a new name in token of the change in Wampanoag leadership and the tribe's continued friendship with the colonists. The English, thinking of ancient Greek history, gave Wamsutta the name of Alexander and awarded his younger brother Metacom the name of Alexander's father, Philip.

The relations between the Wampanoags and Plymouth also worsened because of events in England. In the wake of Cromwell's death, General George Monck maneuvered with key supporters and the general acclaim of London to bring Charles II from exile and restore the monarchy. The Restoration endangered Plymouth because it had never obtained a charter and, like the other New England colonies, its founders had connections to the Parliamentarians who had executed Charles I in 1649. The colony had, in essence, depended on the Wampanoags for its tentative existence under English law, but the tribe's territory formed a border zone also sought after by Rhode Island and Massachusetts. Thus, in July 1662, when Alexander sold land to Rhode Island, Plymouth leaders became nervous and asked the sachem not to deal with anyone but them. But eight days later, he sold more land to Rhode Island. Josiah Winslow, son of Plymouth's governor and commander of its forces, took ten men to force Alexander to come and parley. He found the sachem at the family's summer hunting camp near modern-day Halifax. Wamsutta agreed to go, but once under way he became very sick. Although Winslow quickly released him, Alexander died while on the way home.

Plymouth immediately summoned Wamsutta's younger brother and successor to answer the charges of conspiring against the English. Metacom grew up sensitive to the swelling strength of the English newcomers. He was born about 1640—a generation after a massive epidemic decimated his people and his father became the first ally of the newly arrived Pilgrims, and two years after the colonists had established their power by destroying the Pequot tribe. No doubt thinking of his brother's fate, the new Wampanoag sachem came without being compelled and quickly agreed to a treaty that continued existing agreements with the colony. However, the document also contained a new clause that Metacom would *never* sell land without Plymouth's permission. The new sachem was apparently unaware of this addition, because six months later he dictated a letter to the colony that referred to such a ban lasting *seven years*. Metacom also began looking to regain the sovereignty and land that the colonial leaders seemed determined to claim. Like other Native leaders, he found a useful situation in the growing quarrel among the English colonists in the region and a powerful ally in the new king of England.

Political tensions had been building for several years over the legal powers of the colonies, particularly Massachusetts, including their authority to deal with dissidents as well as Natives. The Bay Colony exiled Anabaptists and other dissenters at the time of the Pequot War and, along with Plymouth, passed various laws aimed at Quakers after they began arriving from England

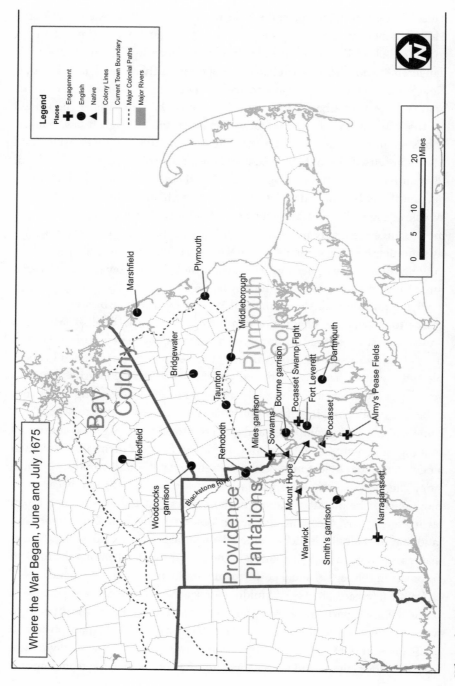

Where the War Began, June and July 1675

in 1656. Massachusetts hanged three Quakers who insisted on returning from exile to preach openly, and Plymouth barred Quakers from entering or holding meetings in the colony; these laws were tightened further between 1658 and 1661. In response, dissenters and entrepreneurs established settlements in neighboring Rhode Island, obtaining deeds from Native sachems, and after the Restoration unleashed a torrent of complaints against the Puritan leaders and endangered the authority and existence of Massachusetts, Plymouth, and Connecticut.

Ignoring the pleas of loyalty by Boston and Plymouth, as well as the immediate repeal of anti-Quaker laws by the latter, King Charles II dispatched a royal delegation to the region in 1664. The committee's official task was to inspect the situation in the region, but everyone knew that it would also compel the Bay Colony to stop persecuting dissenters, particularly since its members were known to dislike Puritans. Once the delegation arrived, it became clear that they were going to focus the King's wrath on Massachusetts, and that the other colonies, settlers, and tribes would be viewed as sympathetic underdogs. The Bay Colony's bête noire, Samuel Gorton, came with a copy of the petition that the Narragansett had sent to King Charles I in 1644, submitting to his authority; the commission approved on behalf of Charles II, thereby placing that tribe on par with the other colonies.

While Plymouth seemed to gain the delegation's sympathy, its lack of a charter must have made its leaders anxious, particularly after Metacom obtained the commissioners' support. Although Massachusetts hated this royal exercise of authority, the colony was divided between those who sought to resist or counter the delegation and those who counseled passive obedience and hoped for the king's favor. Connecticut and Rhode Island were more fortunate as their agents obtained new royal charters that gave each more territory: the former gained New Haven and the latter acquired area claimed by Plymouth, including Metacom's home village of Sowams (now Bristol, Rhode Island).

Metacom in Charge and Besieged

During the next decade, Metacom maneuvered to maintain his power even as the Wampanoag tribe splintered under the persistent pressure of colonial authorities and missionaries. In part to retain influence in these treacherous currents, the sachem sold tracts of land to various colonists and English investors. Conflicts over the uncertain borders that followed, however, were rarely settled by colonial courts to his satisfaction. The Indians were also angered by the attitudes and policies of Plymouth authorities, who in many little decisions and actions showed that they felt they had the right to obtain Wampanoag territory and resources at will. In the 1660s, Plymouth expanded existing towns and established new ones, spurning Metacom's protests that the colonists were violating their treaties and his sovereignty, and making his people feel as if they were being cornered at Mount Hope.

Tensions noticeably increased after Plymouth established a settlement in the mid-1660s in Rehoboth just north of Mount Hope Bay, soon named Swansea, and those colonists continued to buy land (from local leader Totomomocke) closer and closer to Metacom's Sowams. This tension resulted from not only the conflict over whether Plymouth or Metacom controlled that area but also the very different ways that the Natives and the colonists held, managed, and used land. One historian notes that Swansea became an obvious target in part because Rehoboth had for years been "particularly notorious among Wampanoags for its trespassing cattle."[3]

Rumors spread that the sachem was conspiring with either the Dutch or the French against Plymouth. When the colony sent delegates to confront Metacom, he denied the story, blamed Ninigret (whom the Wampanoags disliked) for the rumor, and offered to surrender his firearms to the English as proof of his fidelity—which Plymouth accepted and then told the sachem to appear at the colonial assembly's next meeting in June. Metacom appeared and again swore "love and faithfulness to the English, and that [the rumor] was a meer plot of Ninnegrett."[4] When Plymouth officials questioned Ninigret, he denied the accusation.

Without any other evidence, the colony decided to trust Metacom for the moment and to return his weapons while charging him £40 for the investigation. But after he and his warriors paraded through Swansea with their firearms threateningly displayed, Plymouth demanded that the sachem come to Taunton on April 10, 1671. Metacom came with an armed party but stopped at the edge of town, in essence demanding that the colony's officials come to him. Governor Thomas Prence sent James Brown and Roger Williams, and the sachem agreed to meet with Plymouth officials at the Taunton commons if the two colonists would remain with his men as hostages.

At that conference, Metacom found his small party surrounded by a large group of angry Englishmen, and he realized that, in order to escape the situation unharmed and prevent a larger war, he had to finesse their demands. He therefore signed a treaty that, by acknowledging his violation of past agreements with Plymouth, accepted the colony's view that he had been a subject rather than a sovereign, and he agreed to surrender his men's muskets. But everyone in the region recognized that this treaty only sharpened the conflict. Plymouth officials received reports from Natives, settlers near Sowams, and Connecticut leaders that many of Metacom's warriors retained firearms.

Plymouth leaders demonstrated their anxiety by obtaining promises of loyalty that summer from the sachems of villages on Cape Cod and on the west side of the colony, along with their promises to inform the colony of any threat. These treaties were clearly written for the Native leaders: each cited verses from the Bible in proper Christian fashion, and one noted that "wee were like unto wolves and lions, to destroy one another; but we hope and believe in God; therefore wee desire to enter into covenant with the English respecting our fidelity."[5] Plymouth was particularly concerned about the "squaw sachem" Awashonks, of Saconnet. The colony's leaders demanded that she sign a treaty and surrender her people's firearms; expecting her refusal, they began organizing a war party to compel her obedience, but in late July 1671 she came on her own and signed an agreement in which the English promised to "better healp her to keep off" colonial trespassers.[6] Two months later, Metacom was outmaneuvered when Plymouth leaders gained the support of the United Colonies, and he was forced to sign the treaty that made him subject to Plymouth.

Christian Indians

A more subtle aspect of efforts by the Puritans to extend their power in the region was their increasingly successful effort to convert Indians to Christianity. By the mid-seventeenth century, a growing number of Natives around Boston and Plymouth and on Martha's Vineyard were embracing the colonists' religion. For those in Massachusetts and Plymouth, this meant also accepting English culture and the colonists' laws and sovereignty; those on Cape Cod and Martha's Vineyard, in Wampanoag territory, were more autonomous but similarly tended to ignore Metacom's authority.

The process by which many Wampanoags, Massachusetts, Nipmucs, and Pennacooks embraced the English God and culture was driven by the devastating epidemics and other massive changes to their world. Indians and Puritans similarly believed that the supernatural worked in everyday occurrences, and both groups saw recent events as evidence that Jehovah had overcome the native gods and that survival required adoption of the English God. Roxbury minister John Eliot stepped into this psychic gap after learning the Massachusett language, preaching that Indians could find salvation by shedding heathenish ways and adopting Puritan disciplines in order to breathe the rarefied Calvinist air. Eliot has been depicted by historians as everything from a saint to a land-hungry Machiavellian incompetent; the consensus is that he, like other Puritans, was (by modern standards) inflexible and authoritarian and immediately condemned cultural ways he could not understand. But Puritan criteria were high for anyone who wished to be among the ranks of the godly, regardless of skin color, education, or wealth.

In 1646, after Massachusett sachem Cutshamekin spurned Eliot, almost certainly because the missionary threatened his authority, the minister approached Waban, head of the Massachusett village of Nonantum (modern Newton), west of Boston. Waban found the power of Eliot's God attractive, along with the promise by the colony's officials of secure land title for Christian Indian communities. Perhaps because of Waban's interest, Eliot's audiences at Nonantum grew. The missionary began traveling between several Indian groups in the area, gathering converts. Native converts wore their hair like the English and forswore many old habits, from religious ceremonies to body greasing, to demonstrate their ability to walk the Christian path of righteousness. Waban, who led the converts, requested a tract of land on which the Christian Indians could build an English-style town of their own. In 1651, the General Court gave them a tract of two thousand acres straddling the Charles River, eighteen miles upriver from Boston.

The decision to embrace the Puritan message was made within the evolving Indian worldview. When Eliot and Waban developed their symbiotic relationship, both gained prestige and authority. Those who joined Waban's community, which became Natick, had a special status in their relations with colonial authorities. Eliot served as a conduit for material and spiritual power and brought the power of literacy. Yet Native embrace of a new religion was not simply expediency. Many of those most directly affected by the arrival of the newcomers may have converted because aboriginal concepts could not adequately explain or affect the technology, writing, power, or disease brought by the Anglo-Americans. Christianity seemed to offer answers to these challenges. While many Indians were not receptive to the new beliefs, just a decade after Natick's establishment the town was flourishing and boasted its own congregation of "elect" whose members had been formally blessed by Puritan leaders.

Paradoxically, this radical change presented the opportunity to maintain many Native traditions. Natick became Eliot's showpiece and the model for subsequent praying towns. Yet the village contained an amalgam of English and aboriginal customs. The Indians built an English-style meetinghouse, fort, and arched footbridge across the Charles. House lots were laid out for nuclear families in the English tradition, but for the most part these families erected traditional housing instead of English clapboard. Massachusetts appointed Daniel Gookin Superintendent of Indians, to call Native judges into session and monitor their decisions. The praying Indians adopted a legal code that forbade many traditional practices, from premarital sex to long hair and cracking lice between one's teeth. Eliot established a governing structure that reflected the Bible rather than Native patterns, but the new positions were filled by pre-mission community leaders, and those leaders enforced a traditional regard for community peace and stability.

As the population and authority of the Bay Colony grew, Eliot spread his message farther from Boston. Since a number of Nipmuc men from villages west of Natick were among Eliot's first converts, their relatives seemed particularly fertile ground. The tribe's territory between Connecticut and Massachusetts also had strategic importance, as both colonies recognized Indian allies as a means to extend sovereignty. Eliot founded the first Nipmuc praying town at Hassanamisset, the "place of small stones," thirty-eight miles from Boston along the Indian path to Connecticut, where Grafton is today. After carefully separating the converted from the rest of the village, in 1671 the Puritan missionary established the second Indian church there. Three years later the Christian hamlet had sixteen full church members and about thirty baptized persons, and (as Gookin noted) its sixty residents "produceth plenty of corn, grain, and fruit" and boasted sizeable herds of cattle and pigs.[7]

The Pennacooks, whose territory stretched along the Merrimack River into southern New Hampshire, were another strategic group approached by Eliot. The Puritan missionary established the praying town of Wamesit at the confluence of the Concord and Merrimack rivers in the northwest corner of the Bay Colony, where Chelmsford is today. The site met the colony's secular as well as ecclesiastical needs, for during the fishing season "a great confluence of Indians" came from the north, providing an opportunity to extend Puritan influence and religion into a region rich in fur and timber.[8] The Pennacooks retained close ties to other Western Wabanaki groups and often moved between the southern and eastern river valleys and the northern mountains for best access to trade and resources. One drawback for the Puritans was that the Wamesits socialized frequently with their unconverted and "rebellious" relatives.

By the 1660s, Eliot and Gookin had created a network of seven praying towns—Natick, Hassanamisset, Punkapoag (Stoughton), Wamesit, Okommakamesit (Marlborough), Nashoba, and Magunkaquag (Ashland)—that lay along the edge of colonial settlements, and whose inhabitants maintained connections with unconverted relatives who spurned English law. The Puritan missionaries labored with their Native allies to develop networks that could operate independently of aboriginal kinship and political ties. Only Natick and Hassanamisset had churches, so members living in other villages made weekly pilgrimages to one of the two. These praying towns with churches also served to train Indian missionaries loyal to Waban, Eliot, and colonial authorities, whose influence reached beyond the praying towns. For example, John Sassamon taught at Natick before working as a secretary for first Wamsutta and then Metacom.

This expansion of Christian influence, even by Indian agents, was seen by both Natives and colonists as an extension of colonial authority, threatening Native sovereignty and leadership and facilitating English land purchases. This is why Cutshamekin initially rejected Eliot, as well as why in 1674 Uncas warned Eliot not to enter his territory "to call his Indians to pray to God."[9] One year later, Metacom listed his grievances on the eve of war; the political effects of Eliot's efforts were one major concern. The Wampanoag sachem and his counselors "had a great fear to have ani of their indians should be Cal[l]ed or forsed to be Christian Indians," for "such wer[e] in everi thing more mischievous, only dissemblers, and then the English made them not subject to their kings, and by the[i]r lying to [w]rong their kings."[10]

Sassamon Murdered, Metacom Tried

Sassamon would play a particularly significant and unfortunate role in King Philip's War. His parents were among the earliest Native converts to Christianity; they died when he was young and left him to be raised within an English household. He became fluent in spoken and written English, served

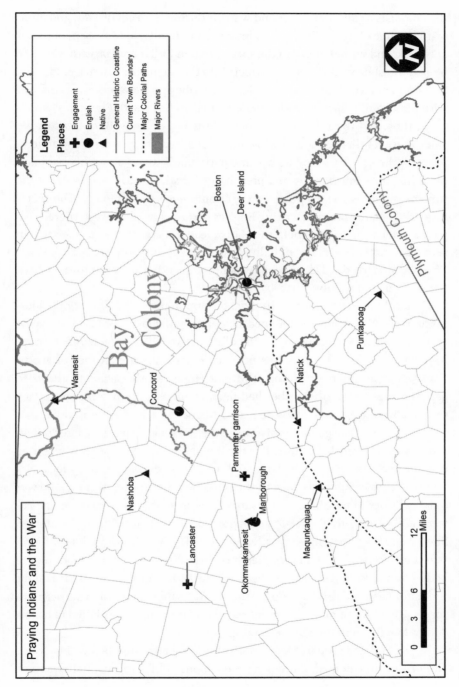

Praying Indians and the War

the colonists as an interpreter and warrior during the Pequot War, and afterward became close to Eliot. He embraced Christianity, became schoolmaster at Natick, and was educated in the special Indian College at Harvard where he helped translate various religious tracts into the Algonquin language. In 1662, Sassamon entered Wamsutta's service as a scribe and translator; he remained with Metacom, helped with the sachem's negotiations with Plymouth, and in 1664, 1665, and 1666 signed as witness to his sale of lands. But Metacom began to suspect that Sassamon was committing fraud to gain land and scheming with the colonists, and he became particularly angry about his secretary providing false information and preaching Christianity to his warriors at the time of the disastrous September 1671 conference in Plymouth. The secretary's skills in reading and writing English certainly would have garnered suspicion even as he tried to help the Native leader. Later that year, the sachem sent Sassamon away. He went to live in a cabin on the shore of Assawompsett Pond in modern-day Lakeville, Massachusetts, and ministered to the Christian Indian community at nearby Namasket.

On a cold January morning in 1675, Sassamon made the fifteen-mile journey to Plymouth. There he obtained a meeting with Governor Josiah Winslow to warn that Metacom was creating alliances with other sachems in order to destroy the English. This was not a complete surprise: stories of armed Wampanoag warriors gathering at Mount Hope and the sachem's efforts to gain the support of other tribes had been common currency for years. Sassamon also told Winslow that he feared Metacom would kill him if his visit became known. The governor dismissed the warning because, he later noted, Indians were rarely believable. But the impact of his message grew when he disappeared less than a week later, and then his body was found by local Natives in February under the ice in the pond near his house. Although he was quickly buried, Englishmen and Natives gossiped about the case. As the rumors and suspicions about Metacom grew, Plymouth authorities disinterred Sassamon's body for a more detailed inquest. The Middleborough jury found that the drowned man had a swollen head, a broken neck, and wounds on the body—all marks that could have been left either by murderers or if he had hit the water hard and drowned under the ice. Yet while many colonists began to suspect that Sassamon had been killed, Plymouth magistrates failed to have a doctor conduct a more complete autopsy.

At the end of February, Metacom voluntarily appeared before Plymouth authorities and denied murdering Sassamon. While the council was not convinced, they lacked proof and let him go. But they did have three of the sachem's counselors arrested as suspects: Mattashunannamo, Tobias, and Tobias's son Wampapaquan. In early March, shortly after the arrests, the Christian Indian Patuckson came to Plymouth and swore that at the end of January he had been standing on a hill overlooking the pond and had seen the three Wampanoags kill Sassamon. On March 1, Plymouth indicted the three for the murder. This trial, which Massachusetts supported, was a direct challenge to Metacom and a clash between Plymouth and Wampanoag sovereignty. The trial took place before the Plymouth General Court, which (as in Massachusetts and Connecticut) had judicial as well as legislative powers. For the trial it appointed a panel of eight judges headed by Governor Josiah Winslow and impaneled a jury of twelve Englishmen, with six Christian Indians who would "healpe to consult and advice with"—and perhaps deflect criticisms that the colonists were treating the defendants unfairly.[11]

The trial featured a mixture of medieval evidence (the coroner's inquest reported that Sassamon's corpse had begun to bleed again when approached by Tobias) and eyewitness testimony by Patuckson. But the tradition of the bleeding corpse was somewhat controversial, and Patuckson's credibility was cast into doubt during the trial when the suspects said that he owed them a gambling debt and had accused them of Sassamon's murder "knowing it would please the English."[12] The three accused men denied the charges. But the jury decided to believe the doubtful evidence and to ignore the biblical standard usually accepted in New England that two witnesses were required for conviction of a capital offense. The Christian Indians agreed with the conviction, and judges sentenced the three Wampanoag leaders to hang.

On June 8, they were led out to be executed. Wampapaquan was last in line, but the rope broke and he fell to the ground. He was encouraged to confess to gain mercy, and in desperation he accused the other two of carrying out the murder at Metacom's orders while he watched. But a month later he was shot anyway. Metacom would later complain that "if 20 of there [h]onest Indians testified that an Englishman had dun them rong, it was as nothing, and if but one of ther worst Indians testified against ani Indian or ther king when it plesed the English that was sufictiant."[13] He also noted that if he wanted Sassamon dead it would have been his right by custom; he did not need to cover it up. This was the first English trial of Indian-on-Indian murder; Plymouth had preempted what should have been a Native prerogative. For the Wampanoag sachem, the trial and its results were a blatant challenge to his sovereignty by Plymouth. Metacom also felt that the prominent role of Christian Indians in the trial was evidence that the colonists would manipulate Natives to dominate and rule the region.

Looming War Clouds

The Wampanoag sachem was already gathering his warriors and seeking alliances with other tribes against the English. The colonists anticipated that he would soon attack; one day, men near Boston heard a gun fire, musketballs whistle over their heads, and drums in the woods but saw nothing; at nearly the same time, men in Plymouth heard men on horseback riding back and forth but saw nothing. Plymouth and Massachusetts began dispatching delegates to other Native communities to seek allies or at least gain their neutrality. The often-personal nature of politics and frontier relationships, as well as the connection between those relationships and state policies, is highlighted by these hurried conferences—which, unfortunately, were only recorded on the English side.

Benjamin Church began his significant role in King Philip's War in that fashion. In 1674 he had built his home at Saconnet, near Pocasset, on the east side of Mount Hope Bay. Church spoke Wampanoag and had developed close relations with Natives living in the area. Plymouth authorities asked him to investigate the potential threat, so on June 7 he went to the village of the Saconnet squaw sachem Awashonks to ask her about the rumors that Metacom was "plotting a bloody design." She introduced Church to six "Mount-hope Men" who had carried the message that the colonists were gathering an army to invade Wampanoag territory and had threatened that if she did not join Metacom's alliance, he would send his warriors to kill cattle and burn houses in colonial settlements near her village, "which would provide the English to fall upon her." Church advised her that "if Philip were resolv'd to make War, her best way would be knock those Six Mount-hopes on the head, and shelter herself under the Protection of the English."[14] This was hardly popular with the Saconnets; at least one of her counselors tried to draw Church aside in order to kill him. After further conversation, she asked Church to negotiate on her behalf with Plymouth and sent two of her men with him to make sure he was not harmed.

But such negotiations were fruitless to prevent the larger war because Metacom and the United Colonies could not agree on whether Native leaders were sovereigns or subjects and whether their people were ultimately autonomous or under colonial authority. On June 11, just three days after the two Wampanoags were hanged, John Brown at Swansea, who had often dealt with Metacom and other Natives, wrote a panicky note to Governor Winslow. The Wampanoags "have sent their wives to Narroganset for safety," he wrote, warriors were flocking to Mount Hope from Narragansett and other places, and the "continued warning of the drum" was audible. One Indian had told him that he had heard that Wampanoags guarded the paths to Taunton and that "the younger sort were much set against the English," and that day another had quit work without waiting for wages "saying he was sent for to fight with the English within 2 days." Brown concluded that Metacom's men were "in a posture of war."[15]

Five days later, John Easton, the deputy governor of Rhode Island, arranged to meet Metacom at a small island in Narragansett Bay to seek a way to prevent the looming hostilities. At the meeting, Metacom and his men charged the English in general and Plymouth in particular with criminal aggression. When Easton suggested arbitration, they complained that English arbitrators inevitably favored the colonists and in the past had allowed them to unfairly take Native lands. But the Quaker official's suggestion of a sachem and New York governor Sir Edmund Andros as disinterested judges mollified the Wampanoags.

Metacom then insisted on listing his grievances. When the English first came, he told them, his father kept other tribes from harming the small, weak party of Pilgrims; now his heirs were being poorly repaid. In 1660, his brother had been forced at gunpoint to travel to Plymouth and had died on the journey, apparently poisoned. More generally, he complained, when disputes arose, the English believed Indians only when it suited them, and when a sachem sold land, the colonists always claimed more. Traders sold Indians rum and then cheated them of land when they became drunk; the addicted Natives preyed on the sober to feed their habit. The English violated Native customs by setting up who they chose as sachems. Finally, growing numbers of English cattle and horses wandered into Native cornfields and destroyed their crops.

Easton and his colleagues listened but, reluctant to judge (and perhaps fearful of the armed warriors), responded only by telling the Indians that they should not fight the colonists who had become so many and so strong. The Wampanoags agreed in principle but insisted that the colonists must be as fair to them as the strong Massasoit had been to that first helpless set of English settlers. The current leaders of Plymouth, however, ignored Easton's effort at mediation, in part because of long-standing conflicts with Rhode Island.

On June 19, Winslow sent a message to the Wampanoag sachem demanding that his people surrender their arms and asking Metacom to meet with Plymouth's council. In a reply written by Samuel Gorton, the sachem said he was willing to lay down his arms and go about life as normal, denying any hostile intentions, but warned that any delegates bearing "harsh threats to the Sachim" would face "great danger."[16] Messengers reported to Winslow that the Pocassets and Saconnets had denied that they intended war, but that their warriors were flaunting their firearms and had threatened their English neighbors. On the twenty-first, Winslow contacted his Massachusetts counterpart, John Leverett, warning of the likely war and asking him to ensure the loyalty of the Nipmuc and Narragansett tribes. Leverett also decided to send three delegates to mediate with Metacom—Captain Thomas Savage, James Oliver, and Thomas Brattle—but on June 25, while on the road to Swansea, they found the headless bodies of two Plymouth men, left there as a clear signal from Wampanoag warriors that war had begun.

The War Begins

By the summer of 1675, Swansea was barely a decade old and contained about thirty households living in three distinct villages. Two villages were clustered around garrison houses. One of those was in the northwest part of the town and featured the first Baptist church outside Rhode Island; the minister, John Miles (or Myles), had come from Wales in 1662 to build his meetinghouse and a garrison in the new town. To the east at Mattapoisett (also known as Gardiner's Neck) was the other village, clustered around the Jason Bourne garrison. A third village farther south, on the east side of the Kickamuit River, had about half of the households in the town and lay closest to Metacom's center at Mount Hope.

Swansea was about forty miles from Plymouth, which meant that these scattered families depended heavily on each other and on good relations with the Natives, who vastly outnumbered the English in the vicinity and knew the rivers, swamps, and paths far better. They hoped to maintain those good relations despite the rising tensions. But as John Brown's frantic letter to the governor on June 11 showed, and as a history published during the war noted, residents of Swansea and the neighboring town of Rehoboth (or Seekonk) six miles away became "not a little affrighted" when "several Indians were seen in small Parties" in the area. When challenged, the warriors answered that "they were only on their own Defence, for they understood that the English intended to Cut them off."[17] On Saturday evening, June 19, a group of Wampanoags entered Job Winslow's home on the east side of the Kickamuit River and destroyed furniture and other parts of the house before leaving. The Native warriors did not harm the Winslow family but directed their anger at the colonists' possessions. This frightened and warned Swansea residents of their imminent danger, but without shedding any blood.

The next morning, eight Wampanoag men went to a house at Kickamuit seeking to have their hatchets sharpened. The Englishman refused, saying he would not work on the Sabbath, but no doubt also fearful that the hatchets were meant for him or his neighbors. The men became angry, supposedly telling him that "they knew not who his God was, and that they would do it for all him, or his God either." They left and entered another house and took food, but "hurt no Man." The band then went on to loot various empty houses in the village and set two on fire before leaving. On their way out of the village, the band encountered a colonist on the road; with an apparent sense of humor, the Wampanoags held him for a short time before they "dismist him quietly" after "giving him this caution, that he should not work on his God's Day, and that he should tell no Lies."[18]

Terrified Swansea residents saw these actions as the start of the expected attack, immediately took refuge in the garrisons farther from Mount Hope, and sent word to their governor at his home in Marshfield. He received the alarmed message as morning dawned on the twenty-first and sent word to Bridgewater and Taunton to immediately gather a militia of seventy men, go to Swansea, and raise a second force of around 150 to march on the twenty-second. He also sent word to Massachusetts governor John Leverett, telling him of the events and warning him that the Nipmucs and Narragansetts (who he thought were within the Bay Colony's sphere of influence) might join Metacom but that Plymouth hoped to deal with the problem in just a few days.

The violence was escalating as Plymouth's initial force arrived at the Miles garrison late on the twenty-first. Warriors began shooting at garrison sentries, looted and burned some of the abandoned homes, and killed the settlers' cattle and other animals. John Easton recorded that the first blood was shed on June 23 when "a old man and a lad going to one of those houses did see 3 indians run out thereof. The old man bid the young man shoote so he did and a Indian fell downe," mortally wounded.[19] Tradition holds that this was William Salisbury and his seventeen-year-old son John, who had left the shelter of the Bourne garrison to try to rescue their geese, and that William ordered John to shoot when they saw a group of warriors exiting their burning house. Another version is that John shot when he saw Wampanoags cutting the throats of the family's cattle. Easton went on to note that "it is reported that then sum indians Came to the gareson asked why thay shot the Indian. Thay asked whether he was dead. The Indians saied yea. A English lad saied it was no mater. The men indevered to inforem them it was but an idell lads words but the Indians in hast went away and did not harken to them."[20] This encounter shows that neither the Natives nor the colonists were intent on full-scale war. But this first death opened that door.

On June 24, Plymouth declared a colony-wide day of fasting and humiliation, and with an apparent lull in the hostilities the Swansea residents left the garrisons to pray in nearby meetinghouses. But the relatives of the dead Wampanoag were obligated by custom to seek revenge or compensation for bloodshed, and the "English lad" had seemingly dismissed the matter instead of seeking a settlement. There is also a legend that Metacom was told that he would not win the war unless the English drew the first blood; now they had, and he could now freely send his warriors against the settlers. The warriors waited for the Englishmen to return from church and then struck, killing six, including the two Salisburys, who apparently became the first Englishmen to die in the war. William, his wife, and John had left the garrison to get food and other needed things from their house; the father was shot, and the wife and son were mortally wounded and scalped. In addition to those killed in Swansea at Mattapoiset, near the Bourne garrison, two men from the Miles garrison who had gone out to get water were shot, taken, and later tortured to death. That night at the Miles garrison a sentry was shot and mortally wounded by warriors using the darkness to get closer to the building. The English then decided to send for a surgeon in nearby Rehoboth, but the two messengers were killed on the road; their bodies were found by the Massachusetts delegation the following morning.

This initial violence highlighted what would become key aspects of the terrible conflagration. Initially, the angry warriors seemed satisfied with destroying English property and animals. Such violence was symbolic, meant to express and vent a community's rage; this was also an old English tradition, and Boston colonists would do the same thing a century later to protest the Stamp Act by destroying the homes of Peter Oliver (member of the governor's council and Boston's stamp distributor) and Governor Thomas Hutchinson. The colonists were not surprised that the Wampanoags focused on Swansea, Plymouth's settlement closest to the tribe's center of power and a particularly bitter trespass against Metacom and his people. They also should not have been surprised that the angry Natives focused on the English houses, cattle, and fences, for those were the highly charged symbols of the colonial political, economic, and ecological intrusions that had transformed the area in just a few decades. King Philip's War erupted over sovereignty and power, but it was also driven by deeply conflicting systems of landholding and land use. Finally, the initial human bloodshed was shaped by the demands of Native culture, English settlement patterns, the technologies that both increasingly shared, and the strange relationships between the two peoples, which ranged from fear and loathing to friendship.

Metacom was apparently not present at the initial killings and seemingly was not ready to go to war since he told Easton to pursue the course of mediation. Benjamin Church wrote that, in early June, the Wampanoag sachem had forestalled his angry "Young Men" seeking to kill John Brown of Swansea, who was carrying a message summoning him to Plymouth to answer the charges of having murdered John Sassamon, by promising them "that on the next Lords-Day when the English were gone to Meeting they should rifle their Houses, and from that time forward kill their Cattel." Metacom fulfilled that pledge when he "permitted them to March out of the [Mount Hope] Neck the next Lords-Day, when they plundred the nearest Houses that the Inhabitants had deserted; but as yet offer'd no violence to the People, at least none were killed." Thus, the Wampanoag warriors "began their Hostilities with plundering and destroying Cattel" and not by trying to kill the colonists.[21] Perhaps Metacom was having the warriors harass the colonists to get them to fire that first mortal shot.

The War Spreads

The attack on Swansea began as a local raid, as an effort by some warriors to carry out angry acts of sabotage. That the colonists reacted by fleeing to garrisons, taking up weapons to protect the animals that fed their families, and calling for assistance from outside is hardly surprising, particularly since Plymouth had for years fielded strong evidence that Metacom was assembling an alliance to wage war on them. Unfortunately, their actions spurred an escalation of the conflict, and the killing of the Wampanoag warrior after the first few days marked a clear turning point. Yet even then the clash was confined to the Swansea area and a relatively small group of Natives. Other tribes contacted by Massachusetts and Plymouth told the diplomats that they regarded this as an affair between Metacom and the English. But that did not last. Within a few weeks, the war spread beyond the Wampanoag heartland and involved a growing number of Native and English communities.

One factor was the immediate involvement by the Massachusetts Bay Colony. In addition to sending out ambassadors to other tribes, Governor John Leverett and his council mustered two companies: one with a hundred men from towns around Boston led by Captain Daniel Henchman of Boston, and a second smaller mounted group commanded by Captain Thomas Prentice. Both were sent to Swansea the afternoon of June 26, even before word of the colonists' deaths arrived in Boston.

The three delegates Leverett had sent to mediate with Metacom had concluded, after finding the two corpses on the path to Swansea and talking with the colonists at the Miles garrison, that their mission was impossible, and they headed back to Boston to tell the governor to send troops to help the Plymouth town. The governor and council assembled a third company that evening, with about a hundred more men under the command of Captain Samuel Moseley. This particular band made some uneasy. Moseley was a tough Jamaican privateer (i.e., a pirate with a license), and those who enlisted in his company were described as apprentices, sailors, freed pirates, and servants. Moseley would go on to earn a reputation as an effective officer who was popular with his men but often abused neutral or friendly Indians.

That night, as a lunar eclipse forced the first two companies marching from Boston to pause near Dedham at the Neponset River, those men saw in the strange sky a black splotch shaped like an Indian scalplock or bow. The men talked among themselves and agreed that this was a bad omen foretelling the wider war they feared. Yet after the eclipse cleared, they continued their march. All three Massachusetts detachments gathered near Attleboro the afternoon of the twenty-seventh before continuing onto Swansea, where they arrived the next day.

Combined with the Plymouth force from Bridgewater and Taunton, the

English forces in Swansea totaled over 350, including some Indian allies. We have no idea how many Wampanoags took this opportunity to vent years of anger at the colonial intruders, although they were almost certainly much fewer. Yet the English (who lacked training and a clear chain of command in this situation) continued to be pinned inside the garrisons by warriors who shot from the surrounding woods. Not only was this dangerous and embarrassing for the colonials, but Plymouth and Massachusetts authorities had hoped that their men would quickly defeat Metacom's men and keep him from leaving Mount Hope and joining potential allies. Metacom's men, on the other hand, could take advantage of the bay and rivers to move around the area without problem, and they knew the lay of the land better than most Englishmen.

That first day, the twenty-eighth, after a second sentry at the Miles garrison was hit, some of Prentice's cavalrymen decided (along with Benjamin Church) to seek out and attack the snipers in the woods across the bridge from the garrison that led to Mount Hope. But some warriors were waiting closer to the house, and as the English crossed the bridge the Indians shot and wounded several (including one mortally) before the band managed to scramble back to the garrison. In his self-congratulatory memoirs, Church recalled that after rescuing the mortally wounded man, he stood in the middle and tried to rally his comrades to attack again. While a larger English company tried a badly organized probe across the bridge the next day, a hail of fire forced them back. In the meantime, small bands of Wampanoag warriors made quick strikes at Rehoboth to the west and Taunton to the northeast, up the river with the same name; they burned houses and barns, slaughtered cattle (without taking the meat), and killed a few English. The settlers abandoned both towns, frightened at an enemy who could seemingly come from nowhere without warning.

Finally, on June 30, after Major Thomas Savage had arrived at Swansea with more men and supplies and taken command, the entire colonial force emerged from their garrisons on a full sweep of the Mount Hope peninsula. They found the burned Kickamuit settlement, a set of poles hung with the heads and hands of the captured Englishmen (which was similar to how the colonists dealt with executed criminals), and Metacom's deserted village. His people had withdrawn from the peninsula, apparently the previous evening by canoe, and had disappeared into the swamps and thickets of Pocasset territory on the east side of the bay. Although Church urged an immediate pursuit in order to prevent Metacom from gaining allies and the war from spreading, Savage decided to set up fortifications at Mount Hope and Swansea.

It was not certain that the Pocasset sachem Weetamoo and her people would fight alongside Metacom's warriors. In the first half of the seventeenth century, the tribal bonds that had given Massasoit a large measure of authority over Wampanoag villages and subdivisions as far as Cape Cod were badly eroded by epidemics, the waxing of Narragansett power, and the intervention of English colonists. By the time Metacom became sachem, the Wampanoag villages on Martha's Vineyard were deciding their own conflicts and spurned his authority. The English considered the Pocassets one of the strongest groups in the area; Nathaniel Saltonstall called Weetamoo "as Potent a Prince as any round about her, and hath as much Corn, Land, and Men at her Command."[22] In early June, Weetamoo had told Church that she hoped to avoid war, and her husband would in the end follow his allegiance to the English. On the other hand, the Pocasset and Sowam Wampanoags were neighbors, Weetamoe had been married to Wamsutta before he died, and no doubt many of her people were married or related to people in Metacom's village, all of which created close bonds.

Not surprisingly, she and her people sheltered the Wampanoag refugees and may have helped ferry many of them across the bay the previous evening. Almost certainly she and her counselors immediately met with Metacom and his. They soon agreed, no doubt urged on by her warriors, to join his campaign against the English. Their decision may have been made easier by the colonists' responses, particularly the forces sent by Massachusetts into Mount Hope and, in early July, probing attacks by English companies against the Pocassets. In one such attack, led by a Dutchman named Cornelius, thirteen were killed and eight captured; in another, the company brought back two scalps and twelve captives. Moseley's company discovered and captured a group of eighty Wampanoags, possibly women and children who Metacom had been forced to abandon during his retreat. All of these captives were, a few months later, shipped to Cadiz, where they were probably sold into slavery. In another incident, at a place known as Almy's Pease Fields, thirty-six Plymouth soldiers led by Benjamin Church sought to attack or intimidate the Pocassets, but they blundered into a large force of warriors and were able to escape only when a sloop suddenly appeared and pulled them to safety. The alliance that formed at this time between the Pocassets and Metacom highlights the continued importance of kinship, dislike of the colonists, and fear of unbridled English violence.

Comparing the Combatants

The Wampanoags seemed to face daunting odds against the English, who for decades had worked together through the commissioners of the United Colonies and could potentially assemble over ten thousand men and much better supplies. While the Rhode Islanders were officially pariahs, the colony's leaders had shown that they would support their English cousins with information and provisions. The English were used to a command and control structure that could organize men and materials across a wide distance, whereas the Wampanoags were a loosely knit confederation of villages and kinship groups. Although that tribe may have been developing a stronger leadership structure in the early seventeenth century, it had been shattered by epidemics and English colonization, so Metacom lacked the authority naturally held by an English magistrate or commander.

However, in the initial stages of the war the Wampanoags had the advantage. Both Massachusetts and Connecticut were distracted by other problems: the former had since the restoration of King Charles II faced a series of threats as the new king sought to reduce or eliminate the Puritan colony's autonomy, and the latter found its western areas claimed by the powerful New York governor Edmund Andros. The 1664 commission had challenged the legitimacy of the United Colonies, which meant that even as the organization continued to function the leaders of each member colony had to focus more on provincial needs and ambitions.

Native men were better trained and conditioned for war, and they were trained from an early age to stalk game (including their enemies) quietly and patiently. Their tradition was to capture in order to adopt or torture enemies rather than kill, and to do so quickly without losing any of their own, which meant that they emphasized small, highly mobile groups. Native political customs and military organization also emphasized independent decision making by band leaders. While many rallied to Metacom's side, generally their hierarchy was fairly weak and their war leaders gained authority by their ability to guide successful strikes at the enemy with minimum losses to their men. While the Natives as well as the English faced the threat that their enemies could and would burn their crops or attack the men or women as they worked in the fields, the colonists were aware that their grain mills and cattle were particularly vulnerable targets.

Indeed, most colonists were farmers, and few had real fighting experience. The colonies began with the English militia tradition that all able-bodied adult men were responsible to a local (town) company, led by local gentry often elected by the company. When the fighting began in Swansea, Plymouth sent word to villages near the town to send their companies while the Massachusetts government formed companies from nearby volunteers. But as the war spread, colonies began raising forces by deciding how many soldiers they needed and then assigning each town a quota of men. Most historians have assumed that the resulting companies were cross sections of the population; a recent study shows, however, that in Essex County, Massachusetts, most town committees of militia chose young unmarried men of marginal social and economic status—some committees carefully selected those who had challenged the community or its leaders.[23] Their supplies were provided from various sources, with the expected problems and lack of enthusiasm. While the United Colonies tried to coordinate campaigns, each colony continued to pursue its own strategic and political needs in deciding how to pursue the war.

All of these forces drew on European traditions of disciplined hierarchy, and their sluggish tactics drew the scorn of Indian warriors, as Mary Rowlandson found out in January 1676 when her captors scoffed that any pursuit would not come until the spring. Later in the war, some colonial officers who led small units, such as Benjamin Church, adopted Native tactics of not gathering in a large force and walking widely separated, so that they were less vulnerable to surprise attacks and snipers. But the larger colonial forces were also useful. For example, Church found that the threat of this large force led Wampanoag and Narragansett warriors to retreat into areas where they could be more easily hunted, and then they were more likely to surrender as he approached because they feared that his small company was part of a much larger army.

New England colonists usually fortified at least one large house in the town to create a garrison and stocked it with extra food and water. This was often the house of their minister: it was usually the largest, was built by the town and probably thought of as quasi-public property, and was usually in the center of the town near the meetinghouse. As war loomed and then erupted, many towns took more extensive preparations for defense. On February 19, 1675, the town of Plymouth voted to rebuild its 1621 fort, making the walls ten feet high, one hundred feet square on each side; every man was required to help with construction. Topsfield started on a stone wall around its meetinghouse with a watchtower. Hatfield, Hadley, and Northampton along the Connecticut River rushed to build palisades—tall logs placed upright in a tight pattern with a single entrance that could be shut or easily defended.

Bigger towns such as Hartford and New London in Connecticut had fortified garrison houses, a blockhouse, and a palisade. On June 13, 1675, as tensions increased, the town of Billerica on the northern edges of the Boston region voted to build a "place of safety" in order "to take special care for the preserving of our lives and the lives of our wives and children, the enemy being near." Two months later, after war exploded, they designated eight homes as garrisons and assigned each family in the town to one; the minister's home was named as "ye maine garrison & ye last refuge in case of extremity."[24] Multiple garrisons provided cross fire and multiple zones of defense.

During King Philip's War, the colonists also built forts to control territory and as symbols of dominance, as they had a century before in Ireland. This was why Thomas Savage decided to build Fort Leverett at Pocasset. The Massachusetts council considered abandoning towns west of the Charles River and using that and other rivers, along with ponds and an eight-foot-high wall, to create a barrier against attack by Metacom and his allies. Historians have tended to ridicule this proposal, echoing the scorn that the Indians had for the hesitant English soldiers, and, like Benjamin Church, to be critical of the settlers' tendency to build and man forts. Although writers on Native-colonial warfare agree that fortifications helped protect noncombatants, most emphasize that Natives knew the land and bypassed such obstructions with little problem and much laughter, and that the colonial soldiers who stayed within the walls of a fort had little effect on the war. But there is evidence that strategically placed fortifications did play a significant role during King Philip's War. While Metacom's people did bypass the fort being constructed at Mount Hope, they found it difficult and barely managed to get away with the English in close pursuit. Forts could and did monitor the more manageable routes of travel and communication (roads and rivers), as well as the better sources of food and water.

Natives themselves built fortifications of various sorts. They usually located their villages astraddle strategic paths or alongside rivers. Before European settlement, many tribes east of the Mississippi River surrounded their villages with palisades. It was that kind of fort that the Pequots built around their Mystic village, which the English managed to penetrate and destroy in 1637. Around 1650, the Agawams built a palisade around a large village on a bluff on the east bank of the Connecticut River near Springfield, now known as Fort Hill. Indian forts, like their colonial counterparts, were all over the region, built by Nipmucs, Wampanoags, Wabanakis, Mohegans, and others.

The Indians also rapidly saw the advantage in the more elaborate defensive bulwarks built by Europeans. In the 1650s, Wabanakis living around modern-day Ossipee, New Hampshire, hired English craftsmen to build a fort with walls fourteen feet high as a defense against Mohawk attacks. Not surprisingly, the Natives also learned to build such structures. Many of Eliot's Christian Indian towns built forts around the time of the war; these structures probably included English as well as Native features, since (according to Eliot) the Natick Indians had in the 1650s constructed a meetinghouse and a bridge. In the late fall of 1675, the Narragansetts built a rectangular fort with a tall tight palisade, backed by a clay wall nearly sixteen feet thick, and blockhouses and "flankers" at each corner and vulnerable areas that allowed cross fire. It was built on four acres rising above a huge swamp, with only one approach in normal weather, and held about five hundred wigwams.

Indians and the English both used a mixture of weapons: the colonists had muskets, pikes (spears), and swords; the Natives had muskets, bows and arrows, spears, knives, and clubs. Indian clubs were particularly striking: the one supposedly wielded by Metacom (and now held by the Fruitlands Museum in Massachusetts) has a decorated curved handle and a ball head perfect for shattering bone and skull. The other "primitive" weapons could also be quite effective. For example, the bow and arrow was more dependable than a musket in wet weather and could be reloaded and fired more quickly and quietly than firearms.

In 1675, many of the colonial muskets were still matchlocks, which used a lit string to ignite the gunpowder and were so heavy that a forked pole was used to support the barrel, although a growing number were the faster and lighter flintlocks. Metacom's warriors were rumored to be well armed with the latest flintlocks. During most of the seventeenth century the Natives were largely dependent on Dutch and English traders for powder and shot. But this was changing at the time of the war: in the spring of 1676, colonial militia raiding an encampment at Peskeompskut above Deerfield found two forges used by the Indians to repair muskets and make musketballs. In addition, the warriors' tactics and knowledge of the terrain seemed to compensate for any disadvantage in armaments.

NINE DAYS AFTER METACOM and his village crossed the bay to Pocasset territory, an enlarged force of Wampanoags attacked Middleborough, near the village of Nemasket headed by Tispaquin (the Black Sachem), Metacom's brother-in-law, where Sassamon had taught. The warriors looted and burned most of the town as the tiny garrison of only seventeen Englishmen watched. As with Taunton and Rehoboth, Middleborough remained abandoned during the remainder of the war. During the week, warriors led by Totoson, leader of Mattapoissett and one of Metacom's most trusted war leaders, hit the south side of Dartmouth, which included modern New Bedford, burning about thirty homes and (according to Saltonstall) "killing many People after a most Barbarous Manner." They also again attacked Swansea, this time burning about half the town and killing more of the inhabitants, and managed a quick raid on Taunton as well.[25]

Warriors burned abandoned houses and barns, destroyed crops, butchered cattle in the fields, and killed colonists when possible. The English were terrorized, not knowing where or when the warriors would hit next, and most abandoned these towns. While the colonists tried to bring the Indians to open battle so as to land one decisive blow, the Wampanoags targeted English buildings and cattle in hit-and-run attacks, partially because they were potent symbols of the invaders, and partially because they knew that the colonists were dependent on these vulnerable possessions. As the war spread, Metacom's allies would follow these tactics. After burning Medfield in February 1676, a literate (probably Christian) Nipmuc left a note that "You must consider the Indians lost nothing but their life; you must lose your fair houses and cattle."[26]

three The War Widens

THE ERUPTION OF WAR intensified the scramble to acquire allies or neutralize potential enemies. Metacom had for months sought to establish alliances with other tribes in the region, but as the fighting broke out he seemed to have had little success, and Plymouth's diplomatic efforts that spring forestalled his influence among other Wampanoag sachems and villages. The English were more united: as fellow members of the United Colonies, Massachusetts and Connecticut quickly committed themselves to assisting Plymouth, even though some worried about the justice of the elder colony's actions and thought that they might suffer from the violence. Rhode Islanders were even more ambivalent and also lacked unity: many were Quakers and refused to join the war; however, since they shared the perception that all English were in danger, even that colony provided logistical and diplomatic support. Both Metacom and the English knew that their fate in this conflict would rest on how many other Native groups fought with or against one side or the other.

While Metacom sent delegates with wampum to the Nipmucs, Narragansetts, Mohegans, and tribes farther west, Massachusetts worked to keep the Narragansetts and the Nipmucs friendly or neutral, and Connecticut sought to ensure the continued support of the Mohegans and Pequots. The colonists initially seemed to hold the advantage. Shortly after the eruption of war, most Nipmucs apparently took the path of war against the English, but those that had embraced Christianity endeavored to stay out of the fight or went to join the colonists. More astonishingly, most Wampanoags, Christian or not, refused to assist Metacom; some joined Plymouth's forces, and others agreed to defend their English neighbors if attacked and to capture any Indians who tried to recruit them for Metacom. Uncas and the Mohegans enthusiastically joined the colonial side, and the weaker Pequots offered their services to Connecticut. At first these allies were mostly welcomed, although after war spread to Nipmuc territory Massachusetts colonists began to fear that even those Christian Indians who swore allegiance were secretly joining in the attacks against the English.

In July, the United Colonies had believed that the conflict with Metacom could be confined to the Pocasset peninsula. But in early August, a Nipmuc attack on Brookfield and Metacom's escape to join with that tribe widened the scope of the war. The colonists became even more fearful and besieged when, at the end of the month, Natives in the upper Connecticut River valley turned against the settlers, and a few weeks later Wabanakis along coastal New Hampshire and southern Maine raided outposts and settlements. For decades, Native anger had grown as the English became more powerful and encroached on land and fishing areas. But these tribes finally joined in the war only after the anxious colonists tried to confiscate their weapons in order to *prevent* attacks. Such events made New Englanders increasingly fearful that *all* Indians were openly or secretly allied to destroy them.

Narragansetts and Nipmucs

As war loomed, the English were particularly concerned about the powerful Narragansett tribe. On June 21, Boston dispatched Edward Hutchinson (eldest son of the banished and deceased Anne Hutchinson) and two others to Roger Williams to ask him to again help negotiations; he hastily agreed, and a half an hour later the four were on their horses. They hoped to meet with the tribe's leaders at Wickford along Narragansett Bay but agreed to their request to have the council deeper in tribal territory. At Worden Pond, four Narragansett sachems—Pessacus, Ninigret, Quinnapin, and the "old Queen" Quaiapen—met the English envoys. They reassured the colonists that no warriors from their tribe had joined Metacom, that those who had married into his tribe "should returne or perish there," and that if he or his people came to them they would "deliver them up to the English." But they also wanted to know why Plymouth "pursued" Metacom and, after being told that he had re-belled against the colony that had been "his ancient friends and proctectours [*sic*]," demanded to know why Rhode Island and Massachusetts had gone to help Plymouth instead of letting the two parties "fight it out." Williams's an-swer was that all of the colonies were subject to King Charles, and that all English were duty-bound "to stand to the Death by Each other."[1] Fortunately for the colonists, no such connection bound the region's Native peoples.

Three weeks later, the Narragansetts were confronted by Massachusetts and Connecticut troops dispatched from Swansea following rumors that the tribe had given refuge to some Wampanoags and that some had joined with Metacom's warriors or on their own were robbing English homes. The colo-nies' commissioners, including Hutchinson, Joseph Dudley, and Wait Win-throp, insisted that the tribe sign a formal treaty and send hostages to Boston as guarantees. The Narragansetts replied that they were neutral in the conflict but could not control individuals from their tribe. The English threatened to attack unless they received guarantees of friendship, so on July 15 four tribal counselors reluctantly agreed to a treaty, promising to turn over any of Meta-com's people, return all goods stolen from the colonists, send hostages, and recognize all land sales to the English made by their people. But the treaty was meaningless and tended to alienate the tribe, since none of the Narragansett sachems or war captains were present. Indeed, the Connecticut representa-tives objected to the Massachusetts demand for hostages, noting that the tribe was still neutral and should not be treated as enemies.

The Nipmucs were also worrisome, for they had close relations with the Wampanoags, their villages lay across a wide territory between all of the English colonies, and within their territory Massachusetts had only recently established the towns of Brookfield, Lancaster (Nashaway), and Worcester—which in mid-1675 was only a small cluster of houses. Unlike the Narragan-setts, the Nipmucs had no chief sachem or other centralized political lead-ership; instead, the tribe consisted of widely scattered villages and hamlets primarily connected by kinship and culture. The colonial government also had relatively little experience with the Nipmucs. Massachusetts governor John Leverett therefore asked Ephraim Curtis, a land speculator, trader, and resident of Worcester, who had dealt with the Nipmucs for years, to obtain

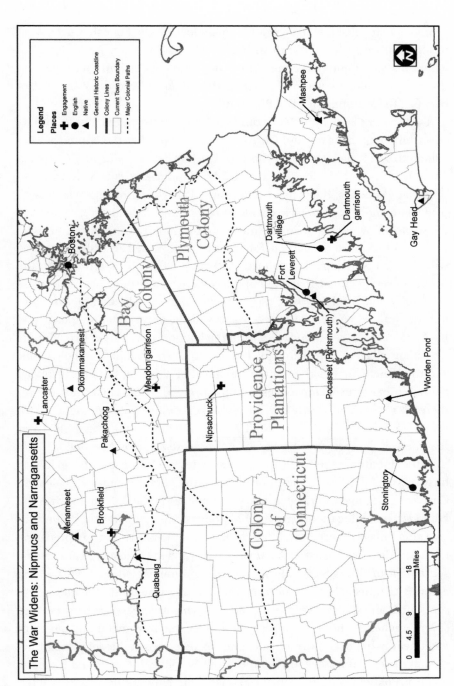

The War Widens: Nipmucs and Narragansetts

promises that tribal members would remain loyal to the English. Curtis went to eight villages and met with thirteen sachems on June 24 and 25, all of whom reassured him that none of their men had gone to join Metacom, and that they remained loyal to Massachusetts and considered the war a matter between the Wampanoags and Plymouth.

Three weeks later, after Metacom's escape to Pocasset, the Massachusetts governor's council again sent Curtis to find out whether the Nipmucs were edging toward involvement in the war. On July 14, stopping at a Christian Nipmuc village in Marlborough, probably Okommakamesit, he heard a report that Matoonas, the constable in nearby Pakachoog, had been seen with fifty Wampanoag warriors. He decided to try to find and talk with Matoonas, but while following a trail he ran into about two hundred angry warriors who nearly shot him and his party before six sachems arrived and, after speaking with Curtis's Natick guides, calmed the young men. Curtis reported to the Massachusetts council that the Nipmucs were "wavering; the young were very Surly and Insolent, the elder ones shewing some Inclination to maintain the wanted peace."[2] Miles away at about the same time, Matoonas and his Nipmucs attacked Mendon (within the bounds of which lay two Nipmuc Christian villages), killed four or five Englishmen working in their fields, and then left. This was the first attack outside Plymouth, the first involving a group other than Wampanoags, and the first led by Christian Indians. Yet there was no evidence that this attack was carried out in conjunction with Metacom, who at the time was still somewhere among the Pocassets. Later that month, the spread of the war led residents to abandon Mendon.

After Hutchinson helped gain the treaty with the Narragansetts, on July 27 he was assigned to lead a delegation, along with Captain Thomas Wheeler and Curtis as guide and interpreter, to try to obtain a similar agreement with the Nipmucs, including the surrender of Matoonas. Along the way they found village after village deserted, which indicated that the Nipmucs were preparing for hostilities. On August 1, the small party reached Quabaug, near the new settlement of Brookfield, only to find that prominent Nipmuc village also empty. Hutchinson heard that the Nipmucs were gathered at Menameset and sent Curtis and several other men to arrange a meeting. They managed to find several sachems who seemed angry and in a dangerous mood but agreed to meet nearby the next morning at 8 a.m. However, when the delegation traveled to the meeting place, three miles from Brookfield, they found it empty. Some Brookfield settlers, convinced that their Nipmuc neighbors wanted peace, persuaded Hutchinson to push on and look for the Indian camp, but as the party went single file through a narrow ravine they were ambushed. Around two hundred Nipmuc warriors poured musket fire from the side as others closed in from behind; somehow, twenty of the twenty-eight managed to clamber up a hillside and get away; Hutchinson would die of his wounds seventeen days later.

The survivors sought refuge in a garrison in Brookfield, where the approximately eighty residents, mostly women and children, joined them to wait for the inevitable attack. Curtis and Henry Young rode east to get help from Marlborough, but they soon ran into Nipmucs and were forced to return. Warriors led by the Quabaug sachem Muttawmp soon arrived, burned the rest of the town, and besieged the garrison. Several Englishmen who exposed themselves or left the garrison were killed; the besiegers cut off the head of one and, to the horror of the helpless colonists, used the skull as a football. Finally, that evening, Curtis managed to escape and ran the thirty miles to Marlborough; the town then sent a messenger to alert Captain Simon Willard at Lancaster about the siege. In the meantime, the Indians attempted various tactics to take the house, such as using flaming arrows to set fire to its roof and then piling hay against a corner of the building to ignite the walls. In both cases, the besieged managed to put out the fires. Then the warriors tried lighting a large barrel on wheels and using long poles to push it against the house, but a fortuitous rainstorm extinguished the fire. Finally, on August 4, Willard's force arrived and the Nipmucs withdrew. After a few weeks, Willard withdrew his men and took with him the remaining traumatized townspeople. Brookfield remained abandoned for nearly two decades.

Whereas Metacom's anger at losing sovereignty, power, and land is easy to understand, the reasons for Nipmuc hostility are not as clear. Certainly they were concerned about the colonists' intentions. The sachems initially told Curtis that they had heard that English had killed a Nipmuc man in the north and intended to annihilate the tribe, and a week later some informed him that Black James, the Nipmuc Christian constable of Chabonagonkamug (modern Dudley), threatened that the English would kill all who were not Christians. In addition to these immediate threats, the Nipmucs would have been increasingly angered by the threat of English land purchases, the growth of the colonial population in their midst, and the disruptive influence imposed by Massachusetts through Native Christian ministers and magistrates.

By 1660, Massachusetts officials and investors were very interested in Nipmuc lands, and by the end of that decade they had carved several large settlements in the middle of tribal territory. One of the speculators who sought more land was Daniel Gookin, who took the lead in establishing and settling Worcester. Unfortunately, the decentralized and fractured nature of the Nipmuc tribe meant that sachems who refused to sell land might end up losing their lands to Nipmucs who were willing to deal with men like Gookin. Another source of friction among the Nipmucs would have been the increasing numbers of Christian members of their tribe trained by Massachusetts. For two decades, Massachusetts Christian praying towns had produced Native missionaries like Sassamon who spread English influence, and the initial wave of those towns lay along the eastern edge of Nipmuc territory and attracted a noticeable number of that tribe—who then sought to create Christian communities and networks within Nipmuc villages and areas. These efforts to convert Indians to Christianity represented a clear threat to the non-Christian groups and endangered tribal sovereignty, family, medicine, and other aspects of polity, society, and culture.

In 1674, John Eliot and Gookin went deep in Nipmuc territory to install Christian Nipmuc teachers and constables in seven villages that were still partially non-Christian. While Eliot protested that "he did not meddle with civil right or jurisdiction," Nipmuc leaders were aware that the Indian preachers dispatched by the Bay Colony worked to supplant Native authority.[3] The threat was territorial as well as political, for the Nipmucs were uncomfortably wedged between the growing population of Massachusetts, Connecticut, and Rhode Island. As the English population around Boston increased, ambitious investors from Massachusetts sought to purchase "vacant" lands between the coast and the Connecticut River. In fact, Gookin during this trip met two Nipmuc sachems who gave him and his fellow investors a deed to land that became part of Worcester. Considering the changes and threats to their world since 1660, the Nipmucs must have been increasingly angered at the Bay Colony's intrusion and expansion. Yet this did not seem a dire, immediate threat. The most logical deduction is that Metacom's effort to gain allies found fertile ground, helped by the rumors that the colonists planned to attack the tribe.

Indian Allies for the English

The Nipmucs were divided, however. Many if not most who were Christians sought to fight alongside the colonists and other "praying Indians." They had committed themselves to the English religion; found success or validation in their new praying towns; and gained support for their community's needs, boundaries, and resources from prominent magistrates like Gookin who could intervene for them within the Massachusetts legal and political system. They also had friends and relatives from other tribes—particularly Massachusett—with whom they had lived for years in Natick and other praying towns, forging a new Christian tribe in the region.

At the outbreak of war, men from Natick joined the Massachusetts force sent to relieve Swansea, including three men who guided Prentice to Mount Hope. Some also helped Curtis and Hutchinson in their three diplomatic missions to the Nipmucs; one was captured in the ambush near Brookfield but managed to escape later with important information. Men from other praying towns also sought to join their English brethren in the efforts against Metacom: on July 2, Governor Leverett authorized Gookin to raise a company to serve at Mount Hope; he managed to enlist fifty-two men, in addition to the Natick and Mohegan men already with the colonial forces, and tradition holds that they acquitted themselves well and brought back four Wampanoag scalps to the governor. Christian Indians would, in fact, become some of the most important and dependable if controversial allies of the English during the war.

There were large numbers of Wampanoags whom the colonists successfully persuaded to remain neutral during the war. This was important strategically, for had these villages become Metacom's allies, not only would he have gained more warriors but his uprising would have rapidly raged across a wider front and posed a greater threat to Plymouth and Boston. In 1671, as the tensions between Plymouth and Metacom grew, the colony had signed a series of treaties with leaders of communities between the colony's capital and Buzzard's Bay; most upheld their side of the agreement and stayed out of the conflict. There were also a series of Christian Indian congregations around Plymouth and on Cape Cod, developed by John Cotton, Richard Bourne, and Indian ministers and teachers, including John Sassamon, separate from those in Massachusetts, which provided a core of neutrality if not support for the colonists. The largest was on Cape Cod, where Bourne persuaded sachems in 1665 and 1666 to grant land for a Christian Indian community that became known as Mashpee. At the outbreak of war, Plymouth ordered Indians on the Cape to move to Mashpee, which could be considered a refuge or a jail. Some of these Wampanoags fought with Plymouth forces; the rest remained safely out of the conflict.

The Wampanoags on Martha's Vineyard, like those in Mashpee, began to embrace Christianity after midcentury, but on that island they vastly outnumbered the few English settlers and retained far more power. They gradually forged autonomous churches with a strong, literate, local Native leadership, and they even sent missionaries over to the neighboring island of Nantucket. By the 1670s, the political and social gap between the Vineyard Indian communities and Metacom was quite wide, and they largely ignored him when he visited to try to enforce a sachem's traditional authority.

The Vineyard Indians, however, were not required by their religion to support the English—after all, some Christian Nipmucs fought for Metacom—and indeed the fears of the colonists on the Vineyard almost drove them onto Metacom's side. When news of the eruption of war reached the island, the settlers demanded that Thomas Mayhew, owner and ruler of the island, send a squad to demand that the large Gay Head–Aquinnah community on the other side of the island surrender their weapons. This would have caused great problems for the Indians, and their sachem and council refused but proposed turning Metacom's men over to the English if they crossed to the island and fighting alongside the English if Metacom's men attacked. The English minority on the Vineyard never again confronted the Indians, and the Natives kept their pledge, even turning over kinfolk to mainland magistrates.

Although Christian Indians were more likely to support the English in this war, shared religion was not a prerequisite. The Mohegan sachem Uncas found this alliance particularly advantageous. In 1636, Uncas had provided important help for the colonists against the Pequots as part of his successful effort to gain power in the region. That alliance remained strong during the subsequent decades, as the ambitious sachem was happy to work with the English against the troublesome Narragansetts, even though the subsequent conflicts between the two tribes and his efforts to gain power over other Native groups sometimes alarmed or angered the colonists.

The outbreak of war between Metacom and the English colonies in 1675 provided Uncas the opportunity to end tensions with the colonists and maneuver against his Native adversaries. On July 15, the sachem met with James Fitch, a local minister who worked with the tribe, and swore his friendship while accusing the Narragansetts of protecting Metacom's women and children—an accusation that the English were ready to believe. But Massachusetts authorities were still suspicious, and two weeks later they demanded that Uncas surrender his arms and his men; the Mohegan sachem sent three sons, sixty men, and many firearms to Boston as tokens of his good faith. From there, they joined a company of Massachusetts men dispatched to pursue Metacom. Uncas would pursue his own agenda throughout the war and maintained his autonomy even as he provided scouts and warriors for the English.

The Niantics and Pequots similarly pledged their "fidelity and good affection" to the English at the outbreak of the war. Their loyalty was surprising: the Pequots because of their earlier war with the English, the Niantics because of their connections to the Narragansetts. But the Pequots had developed good relations with Connecticut, which had allowed two bands from the tribe to re-form on reservations. Some Pequot men formed a company in the force dispatched from Stonington in mid-July to demand a treaty of good faith from the Narragansetts, and they continued during the war to serve in separate companies in various campaigns. The Niantics made their decision for different reasons. Their sachem Ninigret had long been ambitious, like his enemy Uncas: in 1638, he tried to force the Montauks on Long Island into tributary status, backing off only when Connecticut threatened war. After 1640, he took an active part in Narragansett councils; following the death of the Narragansett sachem Canonicus in 1647, he gradually gained power as the Niantics and Narragansetts seemed to merge. A year later the English accused him of trying to kill Uncas and failing to pay the tribute demanded of the Narragansetts. Despite Ninigret's continued enmity with Uncas and further problems with the colonists (on September 10, one of his emissaries to Boston was seized and hung because a colonist thought he had been among Metacom's warriors), the Niantic sachem saw that the best course for him and his people was neutrality—which required professing friendship for the colonists while occasionally meeting their demands.

Wampanoags and Nipmucs Unite

After the United Colonies gained the treaty with the Narragansetts on July 15, Massachusetts ordered its troops to return to Taunton and join with Plymouth's units in an effort to smash Metacom's forces. The English thought that they had managed to isolate the Wampanoags on the Pocasset peninsula and that a quick victory could be achieved so that the soldiers could return home to work their farms. On July 19, the combined forces entered Pocasset. They initially came across a few camps, all abandoned, but as they moved deeper into the cedar swamp, they found and then attacked the Wampanoags. The Indians fought off many assaults, and at the end of the day the English left the swamp having lost between five and ten men.

The colonists' casualties and their failure to strike Metacom's main force led them to change tactics and instead garrison the fort at Mount Hope and build another on the southwest side of Pocasset, which they thought would allow them to cut off and starve out the enemy. Massachusetts withdrew all but a hundred men under Captain Henchman (including seventeen Natick Indians) to supplement the Plymouth men. As noted above, building forts to hem in (or to keep out) an enemy was an established European tactic, and certainly Pocasset was well suited for such a move—and besides, the English had no desire to blunder around in a swamp about which the Wampanoags knew far more.

But Metacom again outfoxed the English. The attack on Dartmouth in mid-July had badly shaken Plymouth's settlers. With the Wampanoags supposedly bottled up on Pocasset, Governor Winslow ordered part of the colony's forces to visit that town as a demonstration of their strength and support. On July 29, the Plymouth commander left only twenty-five men at the Mount Hope fort and took 112 soldiers to Dartmouth, passing through Fort Leverett, which was still being constructed by Henchman's men. Metacom saw and seized the opportunity—indeed, Totoson's attack on the town may have been a deliberate move to draw soldiers away from the area—to escape with Weetamoo across the Taunton River near the town of Taunton and head northwest toward Nipmuc territory. They were forced to abandon around one hundred women and children, who were promptly taken and sold into slavery—an action that became common during the war and may have driven some Natives into more desperate opposition. Messengers from Rehoboth brought word to Henchman about Metacom's passage on the evening of July 30, and the following day he went in pursuit.

Men from Providence and Rehoboth, along with fifty Mohegans led by Uncas's oldest son Oweneco, who had just left Boston, were also chasing the Wampanoags. Early in the morning of July 31, they found and attacked the tired warriors at Nipsachuck (Smithfield, Rhode Island), killing twenty-three, including four of Metacom's top leaders. The Wampanoags took refuge in a swamp—terrain that the English had shown they feared—and waited for another assault. But the Plymouth and Providence forces waited for Henchman's men, and after Henchman arrived he paused, which gave Metacom,

Weetamoo, and their men a chance to get away. Weetamoo and a hundred of her people decided to seek refuge with the Narragansetts and avoid further war. Metacom and his men crossed the Pawtucket River and continued up the Blackstone valley into Nipmuc territory. On August 5, one day after the Nipmucs ended their siege of Brookfield, the Wampanoags arrived at a fort the tribe had built at Menameset (New Braintree, Massachusetts). The English had lost the opportunity to end the war quickly, and Metacom and the Nipmucs joined forces.

Although the English seemed to be lining up an impressive roster of Native allies, only the Christian Indians were truly enthusiastic about their support—and the colonists had suspicions about where their true loyalties lay. During the same period, Metacom gained warriors from the Pocassets and, by early August, forged a strong alliance with the Nipmucs that turned a local brush fire into a major conflagration that from the interior threatened all of the New England colonies. Subsequent operations often joined warriors from the two tribes, led by their own sachems but working together for a common goal.

The first combined Nipmuc-Wampanoag operation was an attack on Lancaster led by Monoco on August 22 that burned one house and killed seven colonists. The English were particularly shocked by this attack, and many suspected that Christian Indians, including Pennacooks from Wamesit, had given important information to the enemy and even joined in the attack. Rumors circulated of Metacom being near Stonington (in the southeastern corner of Connecticut) and at Quabaug. The English were also increasingly suspicious that the Narragansetts were secretly aiding the Wampanoag enemy, as news came from various sources that the tribe was providing refuge for many Wampanoag women and children besides Weetamoo and her people. The colonists saw this as a violation of the July 15 treaty, while the Narragansetts who had kinship ties to Wampanoags were apparently trying to keep family members from being sold into slavery while maintaining their distance from the war.

The War Spreads West

After years of anticipation and fear, war had erupted in eastern New England. But as the initial phase of the conflict demonstrated, this was not a struggle between all Indians and all colonists. Instead, religion, kinship, and community interests determined which side one joined, or indeed whether

one joined or tried to stay out of the way. There were few direct connections between the coastal Wampanoags and the Native communities along
the Connecticut River near Massachusetts towns, and there were no apparent
links between Metacom's people and the Wabanakis in Maine. Yet both the
River Indians and the Wabanakis would become deeply involved in this war.
Some of their motivations were unique, and some were shared with other
Natives who fought the English.

River Indian involvement in the war was triggered in part by English land
dealings in the aftermath of war with the Mohawks. In 1660, a band of Sokokis aided their Wabanaki allies against a Mohawk attack; two years later, the
Sokokis raided a Mohawk village; and in 1663, some Mohawk warriors were
killed by Sokokis near Pocumtuck (Deerfield). Fear of retaliation echoed far
down the Connecticut River, and other communities sought (successfully) to
spurn their Sokoki allies and placate the Mohawks. In December 1663, the
angry Iroquois attacked the Sokoki village of Squakeag (Northfield), barely
twenty miles from Pocumtuck, forcing the inhabitants to abandon the area.
The conflict did not immediately widen, largely because the Iroquois and
Pocumtucks, urged by the Dutch and English, initially sought peace. But
war erupted in the summer of 1664 after the Pocumtucks—for unknown
reasons—slaughtered a group of Mohawk sachems who had come to discuss
peace. By February 1665, the Pocumtucks had abandoned their homes and
sought refuge near the English at Springfield and Windsor.

Over the next few years, John Pynchon, the fur trader, merchant, and land-
lord who dominated Springfield, negotiated with the Pocumtucks for deeds
to much of their homelands. Most in the tribe were probably unaware of the
transactions, and even those like the sachem Chaulk who dealt with Pynchon
viewed the arrangements as a form of joint occupancy that permitted the
English to live in the area. But after 1669, as colonial families began to establish farms and barred the Pocumtucks from resettling their fertile village, it
became clear that the English viewed their possession as exclusive. Therefore,
the establishment of Deerfield in 1673 on the site of the core Pocumtuck village must have been particularly disturbing. River Indian anger at the colonists and their fear of what the future might bring were heightened by what
they heard from the Nipmucs, their kinfolk and trading partners.

In the spring of 1675, Metacom sent wampum to the Nonotucks to seek
their support in the coming war, an overture that probably gained a thought-
ful hearing although tribal leaders preferred to wait and see what happened.

After Metacom's warriors escaped from Pocasset, the colonists feared that the Wampanoags and Nipmucs might target their valley settlements. Pynchon sent for solders from Connecticut (which was much closer than Boston) to help protect the area. Massachusetts also sent soldiers, led by Captains Thomas Lathrop of Beverly and Richard Beers of Watertown, and a company of Mohegans joined them at Hatfield.

Unfortunately, the colonists' fears caused them to create the very situation they hoped to avoid. In late June, when Hatfield leaders heard of the outbreak of the war, they demanded that the neighboring Nonotucks surrender their firearms, although they soon returned the weapons in order to gain the Indians' assistance against the Quabaug Nipmucs who attacked Brookfield. On August 24, acting on rumors from the Mohegans and their own suspicions, they again demanded Nonotuck weapons. That night, the Indians fled. The next day, Lathrop and Beers led about a hundred men in pursuit, but at Hopewell Swamp, midway to Deerfield, they were confronted by the Wabanakis' rear guard. The Indians stopped the English pursuit and killed eight before heading north, probably to join with kinfolk near Deerfield. This incident turned a neutral tribe into a firm enemy of the English and created an alliance among the River Indians against the colonists.

Not surprisingly, the first attack came on September 1 against Deerfield. A large force of Pocumtucks, Sokokis, and Nonotucks raided the small village, killing one man and burning several houses. The next day, warriors surprised and killed eight men farther north at Squakeag and destroyed all of the houses, barns, crops, and cattle that belonged to the sixteen families in the town. The English decided to evacuate that small outpost and sent Beers with thirty-six men on horseback from Hadley. On September 4, as that company neared Squakeag, Sokokis along with Nipmucs led by Monoco and Sagamore Sam set a deadly ambush at the crossing of Sawmill Brook. They managed to kill Beers and about half his men, sent the survivors reeling back to Hadley, and captured several to torture later—one of whom was freed by a Natick Christian and escaped.

Two days after that deadly encounter, Major Robert Treat with a hundred Connecticut men from Hartford evacuated Squakeag, along the way finding the heads of some of Beers's men mounted on poles. Treat headed downriver to Hartford, leaving parts of his Connecticut force distributed in garrisons in the remaining valley communities. In the meantime, the United Colonies had decided to gather a force of five hundred men to guard western Mas-

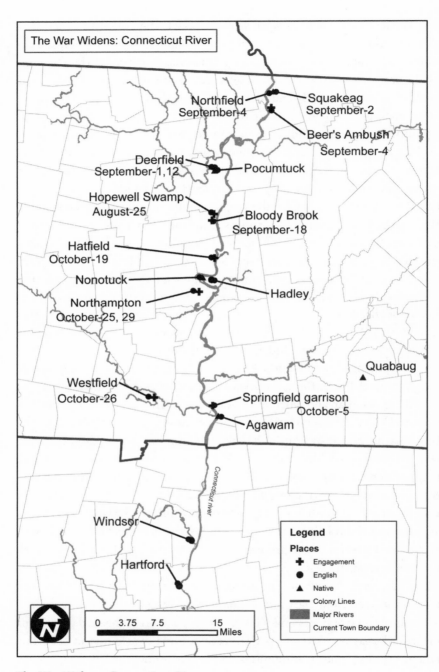

The War Widens: Connecticut River

sachusetts, including the forces under Lathrop and Beers already there, plus additional troops under Captains Samuel Appleton (of Ipswich) and Samuel Moseley. Soon after, Major Treat headed back north along with Mohegans and Pequots under John Mason and arrived at Northampton on September 15. Unfortunately, this only totaled about three hundred men.

Deerfield was hit again on September 12. Warriors took advantage of the Sunday to attack a group of men crossing from one garrison to another that was being used as a church, and they captured one, perhaps to torture later; they then burned two houses, took away loads of meat, and killed large numbers of horses. Militia from Northampton marched north but arrived after the attackers had left. The area commanders decided to abandon the town and sent Captain Lathrop's company to facilitate the evacuation.

On September 18, Pocumtucks and Nipmucs led by Muttawmp launched a devastating attack at Muddy Brook six miles south of Deerfield as Lathrop was leaving for Hadley with eighty men guarding wagons loaded with recently harvested corn. The English dispatched the recently arrived Captain Moseley and his cavalry to scout the area and, based on their intelligence, assumed that no Natives were near; folklore holds that Lathrop's men put their weapons on the carts and were gathering wild grapes along the road when the Indians attacked. The warriors surrounded the wagon train and killed around seventy before Moseley's company arrived in relief and the warriors decided to pull back. But the Natives remained in the area, and that night they taunted Moseley and his men, who had holed up in abandoned Deerfield, by waving the clothing of colonists they had killed. The next day the Indians withdrew, allowing Moseley to return to the site of the battle and bury the English dead, including Lathrop. The battle of Bloody Brook, as the colonists renamed the place, became known as the worst disaster to befall the colonists during the war.

Next was the turn of the largest town in the valley, Springfield. Pynchon, who for decades had dealt closely with Natives in the region, was reluctantly placed in charge of colonial forces in the valley. The neighboring Agawams led by Wequogan had given the "firmest Assurance and Pledges of their Faithfulness and Friendship" to the English, including sending hostages to Hartford and permitting themselves to be supervised by a few local leaders.[4] But English fears increased when Pynchon's mill and a few nearby buildings were burned, although the raiders were probably Nipmucs, who had certainly been operating in the area and may have even destroyed the mill in an effort to spark conflict between the Agawams and Springfield.

Eight days later, on October 4, all of the troops stationed in Springfield headed for Hadley to join with Moseley's unit against Native forces thought to be nearby. That evening, word reached Springfield from Windsor in Connecticut that several hundred of Metacom's warriors had arrived at Wequogan's village and were preparing to attack Springfield. The town's residents went on alert, and the next morning several men who were convinced that the Agawams were friendly went to investigate the rumors. Before reaching the village, the men were attacked; Constable Thomas Miller was killed and Lieutenant Thomas Cooper was mortally wounded but managed to get back to Springfield and gasp a warning before dying.

The warriors then hit the town, burning over thirty unoccupied houses and many barns while besieging the garrisoned dwellings. In the meantime, the Springfield forces that had left for Hadley were returning and the militia from Westfield led by Treat was on the way. Both arrived that afternoon, at which point the Indians withdrew, leaving a devastated town even though only one English woman had been killed and three or four men wounded. Wequogan's assurances of friendship were probably not deceitful; in similar situations, younger men or the women of Native villages compelled the older and more cautious sachems to accept the need for violence.

Contemporary historian William Hubbard, whose account of the war painted the Indians as inferior savages, thought that the Agawams, despite having initially "stood the firmest to the Interest of the English of all the Rest in those Parts," had finally been persuaded by their relatives from the village near Hadley to attack the colonists because "they [were] all hanging together, like Serpent's Eggs" and shared an "inbred Malice and Antipathy against the *English* Manners and Religion."[5] But the truth was more complex. Although the English had initially offered trade and useful assistance against their old enemies the Mohawks, relations had soured as the colonists took more land in dubious deals. English demands that the River Indians surrender weapons and hostages were particularly alarming, because it would have left them helpless against the Mohawks, and because they knew that Plymouth had made the same demands to subjugate Metacom. The arrival of Nipmuc warriors was also a catalyst.

On the English side, the River Indians' deadly attacks badly shook the colonists' confidence. Fears that no Native could be trusted and that all would turn against them became overwhelming. Hubbard wrote that "of all the Mischiefs done by the said Enemy before that Day, the Burning of this Town of Springfield did more than any other, discover the said Actors to be the Children of the Devil, full of all Subtilty and Malice."[6] Massachusetts fears and suspicions were directed toward two Native groups: the Christian Indians from Eliot's praying towns who were strong allies of the colonists and the Narragansetts desperately trying to remain out of the war.

On the day of the attack on Springfield, Pynchon asked to be relieved of command because his severe loss of property and sense of failure made him, as he put it, not "able to attend any public Service."[7] On October 12, Samuel Appleton was appointed regional commander. The English forces that had arrived in mid-September had, along with the abandonment of Deerfield and Squakeag, provided an increasingly effective obstacle to Native attacks, and the River tribes seemed less inclined to hit a colonial town after the initial punishing attack. Perhaps as a result, the tide of Native victories and English problems in the valley slowed. On October 19, warriors led by the Nipmuc sachem Muttawmp attacked Hatfield, but they found the town well defended by Mosely's troops and decided to withdraw rather than risk high casualties for few gains. This was the first time that Natives were repulsed before they could do any damage, and the English celebrated it as a turning point.

Yet this was not the end of Indian effectiveness in the valley. Warriors from various tribes raided Northampton on October 25 and 29, killing two Englishmen and burning four houses, and on the twenty-sixth they hit Westfield, killing three and destroying several homes. By mid-November, the colonists were so dispirited that Appleton had to bar them from leaving the five remaining valley towns. But the Indians were preparing for winter and did not attack again that year.

The War Spreads North

The Eastern Wabanaki homelands featured rich resources for the maritime-based Europeans and were early attractions for investors, colonists, and governments. In the 1620s and 1630s, Plymouth, Massachusetts, and various English and French commercial groups all claimed key sites for trading posts and settlements. Indian deeds became important bargaining chips to key trading posts and real estate. Massachusetts gained dominance in the 1640s and 1650s, displacing Plymouth and British proprietors and creating a few settlements along the coast up to and slightly beyond the Saco River, but these Maine outposts generally operated beyond the reach of Boston's authority.

Since neither Wabanaki nor colonial leaders could command their people—among the Wabanakis by custom, among the English by disregard of custom—reprisals and violence took place in a seemingly unorganized and unpredictable fashion. This lawless situation generated the rising tensions between Natives and colonists in the area that would explode with King Philip's War. Greedy traders were often blamed for the conflict, but part of the problem lay in different perceptions of trade: even in the mid-eighteenth century, Wabanakis demanded consistent prices for their furs, while Massachusetts representatives protested that those prices were dependent on European demand.

Although trade as a cause of the conflict marked Maine as distinct from the other areas of the war, the initial trigger was the same as elsewhere: colonial fears and demands for Native weapons. On July 11, news of the initial violence at Swansea finally reached the Maine village of York. The English residents mustered their militia and marched three days up the Kennebec River to the Androscoggin village at Sheepscot (or Ships Cot) River to demand the surrender of their guns. The Androscoggins, led by Mugg Hegone, tried to pacify the colonists by giving up "an inconsiderable Part of their Ammunition, as a few Guns, a little Powder and Shot, with a few Knives."[8] But the colonists were not satisfied and demanded more.

Native peoples in Maine had become dependent on firearms for hunting, particularly since recent winters had been very hard and agriculture unreliable, and the Sheepscots felt that the loss of those weapons would result in starvation. They consulted their kinfolk and decided not to cooperate with the English. The Sacos were ready to join this opposition, angered by past English violence. A frequently told story is that, shortly before the war began, the wife and infant son of their sachem Squando were canoeing down the Saco River when they were seized by English sailors. Local lore held that Indian children could swim at birth, and the sailors decided to test the idea by throwing Squando's son into Casco Bay, proving folklore incorrect and forever making an enemy of the sachem. When the Androscoggins at Sheepscot refused to send more weapons, and the hostages they had left escaped, English settlers along the coast became worried that the Wabanakis planned to strike.

Not surprisingly, the first sign of Native anger came at the trading post and home of Thomas Purchase, on the Pejepscot River (modern Topsham).

One Androscoggin later complained that "he had given an hundred Pounds [worth of furs] for Water drawn out of Mr. Purchase his well."[9] On September 5, while Purchase and his sons were away, a band of Wabanakis gained entrance to the house with "fair Words, and spake of Trading." They stripped the Purchases of "strong Liquor, and Ammunition," killed a calf and some sheep, and destroyed a feather bed, but "offered no Incivility to the Mistress of the House" and left without harming anyone but threatened that others would soon "deal far worse" with the family.[10]

Four days later, three Penobscots knocking on the door of an English home on the north shore of Casco Bay were fired on by an edgy group of passing Englishmen. One was killed and one wounded. Fortunately for the English, the Penobscots decided not to seek revenge and instead headed north out of harm's way. But within a few days the Androscoggins, Sacos, and other Wabanaki warriors attacked various settlements along Casco Bay and farther south.

The northern front of King Philip's War exploded on September 12 when warriors attacked the Wakely home at Falmouth (modern Portland). The Wabanakis took out their anger on the unfortunate family. A neighbor, George Ingersol, reported that the next day, after assembling a company of Casco militia, he found the bodies of the elderly Thomas Wakely and his wife "halfe in, and halfe out of the house neer half burnt. Their own Son was shot through the body, and also his head dashed in pieces. This young man's Wife was dead, her head skinned." She was "bigg with Child," and two of her children were nearby, their "heads dashed in pieces."[11] The raiders took eleven-year-old Elizabeth Wakely captive; she would be returned the next spring. Other colonists at Falmouth had upbraided Thomas Wakely for building so far from his neighbors, and he had refused to abandon that home when news of the raid on Purchase's trading post created an alarm in the area. His family paid the price along with him.

The attack on the Wakely house generated a panic among the English in the area, who sensibly fled south to take refuge in Major William Philip's garrison house on the west side of the Saco River. On September 18, a large war band burned John Bonython's home on the east side of the Saco and then attacked Philip's place, burning his mills and all of the nearby abandoned homes and nearly taking the garrison. At one point the besiegers loaded a cart with gunpowder, straw, and bark and tried to push it against the house with twenty-foot poles, much as the Nipmucs had tried two months earlier in

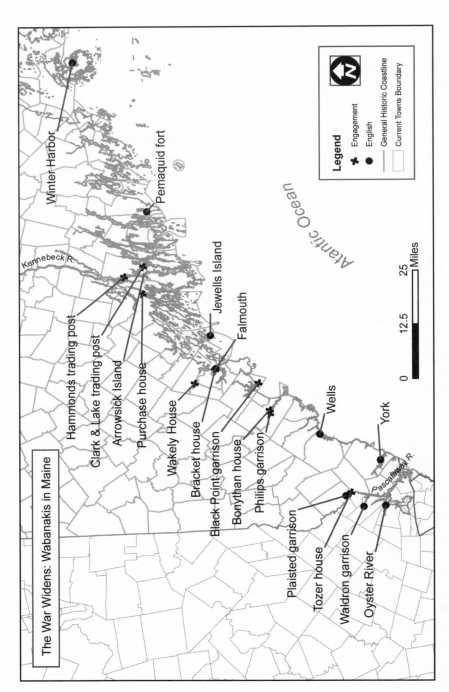

The War Widens: Wabanakis in Maine

Brookfield. There a sudden downpour had extinguished the blaze; this time the attackers were forced to end the siege when the cart stuck and those pushing it were shot by the English in the garrison.

Wabanakis also came south on the Pascataway River, hitting an outpost at Oyster River (Durham, New Hampshire), burning two houses, killing two settlers, and capturing another; a few days later, they killed five English along the Saco River. The English were terrorized as the Natives reasserted control of the region, killing or capturing travelers and farmers working in their fields. The colonists abandoned Winter Harbor, and when a company of militia landed there they were hit hard, with more than a dozen killed.

The Androscoggins moved on to raid larger towns in southern Maine. On October 1, a band led by Hope Hood attacked Richard Tozer's home at Salmon Falls (modern Berwick). A woman saw the warriors at the last minute, shoved the door closed, and blocked it with her weight; they chopped it apart and struck her down, but that gave most of the others in the house (except for two young children) time to escape to a more secure garrison. The raiding party moved on, and most of the English abandoned the settlement, although Tozer and his son remained. The elder Tozer was killed and the son captured two weeks later at their home when about a hundred warriors again attacked Salmon Falls; several other militiamen were killed when they attempted to go to their aid.

A few days later, Lieutenant Roger Plaisted and two of his sons were killed defending a neighboring garrison. The Wabanakis continued their hit-and-run attacks on the English, forcing the settlers to gather in a few garrisons in each town and to abandon houses, barns, and crops, all of which the Natives burned. Small groups of warriors seemed to be everywhere; one hit Black Point (Scarborough, Maine), destroying seven homes and killing several settlers. Finally, a large party raided Wells, killing three and burning a house. As November ended, the Wabanakis left for their winter villages, leaving eighty colonists dead, many houses burned, "all the Plantations about *Pascataqua* [filled] with Fear and Confusion," and the English tide of expansion blunted.[12]

Tensions with Christian Indians

Initially colonial authorities welcomed the loyalty and assistance of the Christian Indians, but many of the English distrusted the Native men in their midst. Daniel Gookin found that during the expedition against Metacom at Mount Hope, "some officers and soldiers in the army who had conceived much animosity against all Indians" charged the Indian soldiers with having been "cowards" who "skulked behind trees in [the] fight" and "shot over the enemies' heads."[13] At the end of July, half of those serving were sent home, and the rest disbanded and went home after joining in the army's pursuit of Metacom from Pocasset in early August; the Massachusetts forces refused to employ more Indians until April 1676, at the low point of the war for the English. The Nipmuc attacks on Mendon and Brookfield, Metacom's escape from Pocasset, and subsequent raids by warriors from both tribes made the colonists increasingly suspicious that all Indians were conspiring against the colonists.

The situation became particularly heated after August 22, when warriors led by the Nipmuc sachem Monoco raided Nashaway (Lancaster), killing seven in the young town near the Nipmuc praying towns and about thirty miles from Boston. Massachusetts colonists became convinced that the Christian Natives in their midst were harboring, selling arms to, or even joining their kinfolk in these attacks. "The clamors and animosity among the common people," sighed Gookin, "increased daily."[14] On August 30, the Governor's Council reluctantly confined all "friend" Indians to the five initial (and most easterly) praying towns.

The same day, Captain Moseley arrested fifteen Christian Indians at Okommakamesit and accused them of taking part in the attack on Lancaster. Two were from Natick, including Abraham Speen, whose family had deeded the land for that town. Moseley tied one (David) to a tree and pretended to be about to shoot him in order to extort his "confession" of carrying out the Lancaster raid. He then tied the fifteen neck to neck and dragged them to Boston for trial, where they were almost lynched before David renounced his confession and other evidence appeared that cleared the arrested men. But since Okommakamesit was not one of the five approved towns, the Indians had to abandon the village. Over the next few months the colonists confiscated or destroyed tools, cattle, crops, and other property at all of the abandoned praying towns.

The animosity of the people of Massachusetts toward Indians was not directed solely at those who were Christians. In early September, Ninigret sent eight delegates to Boston; two colonists grabbed one because they thought he had fought with Metacom, and the town hung him two days later. The colony's

authorities were forced to arrange special protection for Ninigret to come to
Boston, so they could tell him to surrender Weetamoe and other Wampanoags who had fled Pocasset with Metacom but then had sought refuge with the
Narragansetts. He apparently agreed and left relatives as hostages, but after
returning home he managed to avoid this violation of Native traditions and
got the hostages returned at the end of September. Anti-Indian rage was noticeably less potent in the other colonies. The Mohegans and Pequots did not
engender the same hostility in Connecticut, and the Wampanoags on Cape
Cod in Plymouth and on Martha's Vineyard and Nantucket only encountered
some initial English enmity. This relative equanimity ensured that various
tribes who could have given significant support to Metacom and the Nipmucs
remained out of the conflict—a clear if not critical gain for the English.

As Wabanakis joined the war against the English, and settlements from
Springfield to Salmon Falls reeled under the attacks of Natives the colonists
had considered friends, Massachusetts authorities became more sympathetic
to hostility against the Christian Indians. At the end of July, as the Wampanoags fled Pocasset, Wannalancet, son of Passcanoway and sachem of the Pennacooks at the "praying town" of Wamesit, decided "it best prudence" to go
with kinfolk north to the head of the Connecticut River "until the wars were
abated." About 145 remained in Wamesit, one of the five "approved" towns:
most were women, children, and elderly.

On October 18, after a haystack was burned in Chelmsford, the Governor's
Council ordered the arrest of Wamesit and Punkapoag men; the Punkapoags
were quickly released, but the Wamesits suffered several days of imprisonment in Charlestown. After their return, Wamesit was raided in mid-November by fourteen colonists who burned homes and crops, killed a young
man, and wounded five others. Most of the survivors hurried north to join
Wannalancet, sending back word that "there is no safety for us" among the
English. More went north in early February after they were again threatened
by their English neighbors. The six elderly Pennacooks who remained were
soon after burned alive in their wigwam by "some cruel and wicked men, in
a secret manner."[15]

For several weeks in October, the General Court considered taking the
Christian Indians and putting them under guard somewhere closer to Boston,
but no other town was willing to take the Natives. Finally, on October 30,
four days after a shack burned in Dedham, next to Natick, the two hundred
Natives from that praying town were sent to Deer Island in Boston Harbor.

That site was owned by the merchant Samuel Shrimpton, who allowed the Natives to be kept there (in what amounted to a concentration camp) on the conditions that they not cut down the trees or harm his sheep. While the Natick Indians did not resist this removal, they feared (as they told John Eliot, who met them at the dock from where they were to be shipped to the island) that they would be sold into slavery in the Indies—a death sentence. In late December, when Daniel Gookin went with John Eliot to Deer Island, he found that the Indians had little corn other than a small amount sent from Natick and were forced to live "chiefly upon clams and shell-fish, that they digged out of the sand, at low water"; in a subsequent visit he noted that this diet "did occasion fluxes and other diseases among them." Conditions on the island were very bad: the place was "bleak and cold, their wigwams poor and mean, [and] their clothes few and thin."[16]

The Christian Indians were also harassed by their Native cousins. In early November about three hundred Nipmucs entered Hassanamisset, where about 50 men and 150 women and children were building barns and harvesting their crops. The warriors, some of whom were relatives of those in the village, told the Hassanamissets that they "wanted them to go with them quietly, then they would spare their lives; otherwise they would take away all their corn, and then they would be famished." The warriors also told their cousins that those who sought refuge with the English would probably instead be sent "to some Island as the Natick Indians are, where you will be in danger to be starved with cold and hunger, and most probably in the end be all sent out of the country for slaves." As Gookin noted, these Christian Indians had good reason to believe this warning, since among them were eleven who had been arrested at Okommakamesit and so badly treated in Boston. Their "chief ruler" Captain Tom (Wuttascomponom) and "most of the rest" decided that the English had betrayed them and so went willingly; a few others went "with heavy hearts and weeping eyes," particularly the minister Joseph Tukapawillin and his father. But two men, James Speen and Job Kattenanit, had been working at a distance, ran to Mendon, and reported what they had witnessed.[17]

As even the Nipmucs allied with Metacom knew, conditions were bad for the Indians on Deer Island, but they would get worse as winter set in and more Indians were sent there. In December, the Punkapoags were taken from their town and packed off to the island. Initially the Council sent the Nashobas (twelve men and forty-six women and children) to nearby Concord, where John Hoare agreed to house and guard them day and night. But, as

Gookin noted, some in the town joined in the "spirit of animosity and distaste against all Indians" and sent word to Moseley, who had developed a considerable reputation as an Indian hater.[18] While Hoare tried to pacify the captain, after waiting a day Moseley had his men break down the door and force the Indians to Boston after stealing their food, clothing, and other things. While this violation of the Council's orders caused some scandal, none in the General Court wanted to take the Indian side of any controversy, and so in February the Nashobas were also sent to Deer Island, raising the Native population on the island to 550. Despite English hostility and abuse, Indian men on the island clamored to help in the war against Metacom, showing their deep loyalty to the Christian colony, an older dislike of the Wampanoags, or perhaps a strong desire to escape conditions on the island. At various points, up to six men went out on spying or scouting missions. In late spring, when the General Court finally approved large-scale Native enlistment, about one hundred Indian men contributed their critical scouting skills to the colonial victory.

War with the Narragansetts

At midday on Sunday, December 19, 1675, the Narragansett sachem Canonchet may have been walking the perimeter of the huge stronghold that his people had constructed deep in the Great Swamp (modern South Kingston, Rhode Island) as a refuge from the English. It was bitterly cold, and a fierce storm had blown into the area that would by the end of the night dump nearly three feet of snow in the area. Or the cold and snow may have led the thirty-two-year-old sachem to seek shelter in his wigwam, perhaps after getting some succotash (stew) simmering in an iron pot over a fire. Canonchet was the youngest son of Miantonomi, was apparently born just before his father's execution, and became the acknowledged leader of the tribe in the autumn as negotiations faltered with the United Colonies, perhaps because he was already recognized as an outstanding war chief. The Narragansetts had built this European-style fort in the swamp because they knew the territory and because the English had demonstrated over and over again their reluctance and incompetence in fighting in swamps. Perhaps as Canonchet inspected his people's preparations he thought about the four decades of their edgy relationship with the United Colonies that had veered between friendship and war.

When war erupted in June 1675, the tribe tried to remain neutral despite decades of still-smoldering resentments against Massachusetts and Connecticut. They were apparently divided between the younger war hawks who wished to join Metacom against the arrogant Puritans and those who followed the more cautious elder sachems. In their June 25 meeting with Roger Williams and the three Massachusetts delegates, the tribe promised to stay out of the war. But English fears were heightened when a hundred armed Narragansetts went into Warwick, although the warriors quickly left without incident. Even Williams became convinced, three days after the initial raid on Swansea by Metacom's warriors, that Narragansett reassurances of friendship had been "but Words of Policie, falshood, and Treacherie." In mid-July, the United Colonies sent an army to intimidate the tribe and forced several counselors to sign a treaty agreeing to surrender any Wampanoags and to "use all Acts of Hostility" against Metacom.[19] But after escaping from the English encirclement of Pocasset, Weetamoo and many of her people obtained shelter with the Narragansetts, and at various points in the late summer and early fall the colonists heard that the tribe was providing a refuge for the enemy and that some Narragansett warriors had been glimpsed among Metacom's forces.

The Narragansetts still hoped to remain neutral, although that ground became increasingly shaky as the war expanded. On October 11, Roger Williams met with Canonchet and warned him that Metacom would lose the war and that the English would destroy any who helped him. Canonchet in turn told Williams that he wanted peace but could not control his warriors, and that the English needed to fortify and guard their homes. A week later, Canonchet and other Narragansett sachems went to Boston and signed an agreement to continue the peace and to turn over by October 28 any and all Wampanoags among the tribe. But for decades the United Colonies had suspected the Narragansetts of duplicity, and that tribe in turn had many reasons to be angry at the Puritans' overbearing actions. It is entirely likely that, despite the protestations of tribal leaders, many Narragansett warriors would have joined the fight against the Puritans, and as the United Colonies' deadline to turn over Wampanoags approached, tribal leaders made it clear that they would not betray their traditional obligations to kinfolk and rules of hospitality. The United Colonies would not allow the tribe to remain neutral, given their many worries and potential threat (and the attraction of their land), and therefore decided to take preemptive action.

On November 2, just a few days after the second River Indian attack on

Northampton, the Commissioners of the United Colonies meeting in Boston passed a resolution accusing the tribe of being "deeply accessory in the present bloody outrages of the Barbarous Native; That are in open hostilities with the English."[20] Five weeks later, on December 9, after recalling many of their forces from the Connecticut River valley, the Massachusetts Council gathered 527 soldiers led by Samuel Appleton for the campaign. The Council promised their soldiers "that if they played the man, took the Fort, & Drove the Enemy out of the Narragansett Country, which was their great Seat, that they should have a gratuity in land besides their wages."[21] South of Boston, they joined with 159 Plymouth troops, and Plymouth governor Josiah Winslow took command as the joint force gathered at Richard Smith's trading post in Wickford. By December 15, the Narragansetts knew about the army. Stonewall John (a name given him by the English for his skills as a mason) appeared at Wickford, probably sent by Canonchet as a spy and an emissary. He told Winslow of the tribe's desire to maintain peace and boasted of "their Numbers and Strength . . . that the English durst not fight them."[22] At about the same time, just nine miles south, some Narragansetts attacked and overwhelmed Jerry Bull's stone garrison on Tower Hill (Narragansett, Rhode Island), killing seventeen colonists.

But Canonchet may not have known that, by December 19, the colonial army had grown even larger and was approaching his supposedly hidden fort. The day before, the troops rendezvoused with Connecticut forces led by Robert Treat, including 300 English and 150 Mohegans and Pequots. They met at the Bulls' burned-out garrison. The combined army totaled about 1,150 men, the most formidable force ever assembled by the New England colonies. While the English were already short on supplies, they were advantaged by the long cold that had frozen the marshy swamp surrounding the fort such that their soldiers could easily march across the terrain that before had served as a barrier. They were also being led by a Narragansett, Peter, who had been captured on the thirteenth along with thirty-five others by an advance party led by Captain Samuel Mosely and including Benjamin Church. Peter had developed, as Hubbard wrote, "some Disgust with his Country-men, or his Sachim, which made him prove the more real Friend to our Forces in the Service."[23]

Before sunrise, the English headed for the Great Swamp, seven or eight miles away, arriving at its edge around noon. There they exchanged fire with warriors stationed outside the fort and found that the dreaded mire had fro-

ADVENTURES OF THE EARLY SETTLERS OF NEW ENGLAND.   33

CAPTURE OF THE INDIAN FORTRESS.

United Colonies army attacking the Narragansett fort, December 19, 1675. The drawing shows the sophisticated fort built by the Narragansetts, the difficulty faced by the attacking English, and the critical role played by the frozen swamp and the fallen tree, which together facilitated the colonial attack. Illustration in "Adventures of the Early Settlers of New England," *Harper's Weekly* (June 1857), 33. Courtesy Library of Congress.

zen solid. Peter led the English to what he told them was the weakest part of the fort: a six-foot-wide access left by a "Place of Water" across which lay a single huge tree trunk at the height of a man's head.[24] At first the Narragansetts resisted successfully, driving back the attackers and killing two captains. But the English made another attack and got inside the palisades, so the fighting shifted to the narrow spaces between wigwams. Native and English warriors nearly blinded by the driving snow fired at each other at close range, sometimes retreating, other times advancing. Baskets of food piled outside wigwams served as breastworks. Finally, some of the colonial officers persuaded their superiors to set fire to the village, as their fathers had done to the Pequots, killing those trapped inside wigwams. Large numbers of warriors slipped out of the fort, so that most of the 150 Indians who died were probably women, children, and the elderly. The English were badly mauled, with 210 killed or badly wounded. Church and thirty others pursued, but they were soon forced back. The colonial force began to leave the smoldering fort at 4 p.m. and regrouped at Wickford by 2 a.m. the next morning.

Several hundred angry Narragansetts managed to escape. Those warriors brought an intense desire for revenge to the swelling forces against the English, although they suffered from a lack of gunpowder and other supplies. Narragansett and English representatives met several times afterward to discuss a settlement, but those talks had little hope of success as both sides seemed determined to regroup and prepare for another battle.

On January 27, one month after the English attack on the Narragansett fort, Canonchet and his warriors emerged from a hidden camp in Misnock Swamp (modern Coventry, Rhode Island) and attacked Pawtuxet (parts of modern Cranston and Warwick). They burned buildings, killed livestock, and stole supplies before heading off to join the Indian forces camped along the slope of Mount Wachusett in central Massachusetts. A United Colonies force of 1,400 led by Winslow followed to try to bring the Narragansetts to open battle, but the Natives knew the territory too well. A series of costly skirmishes and lack of preparation left the provincial forces discouraged and near starvation; on February 3, Winslow abandoned the chase and brought his troops back to Boston. Once at Wachusett, with Metacom away seeking Mohawk help, Canonchet became the most influential war leader among the swelling force of Natives fighting the Puritans.

four Indians Ascendant

As the winter deepened and then moved into spring, Metacom's allies at Wachusett struck hard at towns in eastern Massachusetts and Plymouth. In February, large forces surprised Lancaster and Medfield, leveling both, and in March, more easterly towns and garrisons nearer Boston were burned, including Marlborough and Providence. The warriors and their leaders exulted that they were finally hitting back at the obnoxious, interminable English and their insufferable cattle. Seemingly unable to stop the assault, and fearful of being burned and scalped, many settlers abandoned the more inland towns and fled to Boston or Salem. The colonists feared that God was using the savages to chastise His people for their sins; this issue and the events of the war became a staple for New England sermons, pamphlets, and books, many of which were published in England even as the conflict continued. Yet colonial leaders were hesitant to ask for assistance from England or from New York for fear that the king or his royal governor would use the war to take control. They also lacked unity: towns were reluctant to send men to fight, each colony had its own needs, and the settlers abused the Christian Indians who were eager to provide desperately needed assistance. In April, bands of enemy warriors moved seemingly at will throughout the countryside; on April 21, a large force nearly destroyed Sudbury, less than twenty miles from Boston.

But the Sudbury fight proved to be the Indians' high-water mark. Even as Metacom's allies continued to burn colonial towns, the tide of the war turned decisively for the English. In February, the Mohawks (at the behest of New York's governor) attacked Metacom and decimated his Wampanoag forces. Beginning in April, the colonists captured important Indian war leaders, coordinated campaigns involving several armies, successfully resisted several Native attacks, created small units that copied the best Indian guerrilla tactics, and (particularly in those units) used many more of their Native allies regularly and more effectively. The Indians were increasingly dogged by famine and disease and faced growing shortages of firearms and ammunition, as nearly all gunpowder was imported from England. The Indians were unable to *destroy* the colonists and seemed to have no other clear goal. Finally, dreaded Mohawk raiding parties began to move through central and eastern Massachusetts, terrorizing the colonists' enemies (and some of their friends). Morale plunged among Metacom's allies and internal discord increased as the war seemed increasingly pointless and hopeless. By June, the forces gathered at Mount Wachusett and near Peskeompskut on the Connecticut River had broken up, and the English began to hunt down the separate groups.

A Scouting Mission

In the wake of the Great Swamp Fight in December, the Massachusetts Council decided to recruit two Native men from Deer Island to scout out the enemy. James Quannapohit and Job Kattenanit of Hassanamisset volunteered, were promised £5 apiece, and were taken from the island and briefed at Daniel Gookin's house in Cambridge. On December 30, the two were ferried up the Charles as far as the falls at Newton and sent on their mission. They went from one abandoned praying town to another: the first night at Natick, the second at Hassanamisset, and the third at Manchage. On the fourth day, they traveled ten miles more, until they found seven "enemy Indians" at Maanexit.

Unaware of the two men's mission or loyalties, their fellow Nipmucs took them first to Quabaug, and then finally on January 4 to the large encampment of Nipmucs (including most of the Hassanamissets) "and divers others" at

Menumesse (modern New Braintree) near Mount Wachusett.[1] The two spies found out that these warriors had recently received messengers from the Narragansetts "declaring their desire to join with them and Philip," but that the Wampanoag sachem and his men were wintering a half-day's journey north of Albany, New York, and were not yet aware of what had transpired at the Swamp Fight.[2] The River Indians had gone to a winter village near Squakeag, halfway between the Nipmucs and Metacom.

The spies saw several things that would augur the course of the war over the next few months. The anticipated arrival of the Narragansetts had made their Nipmuc cousins more confident in their ability "to deal with the English," and they "gloried much in their number and strength."[3] They told Quannapohit that they had captured some weapons in past battles, had traded for some from the Wappingers and Mohawks in the Hudson River valley, had a skilled gunsmith working with them, and expected to get more firearms from the French. Furthermore, in a glimpse of what would doom the Native war effort, they noted that the Nipmucs were eating primarily venison and some corn, pork, and beef taken from a couple of praying towns, and that their main hope for more corn was the raid that they were planning against Lancaster (formerly Nashaway), a small village twelve miles northeast, which lay along the outer boundary of settlements in eastern Massachusetts. They would then seek "to burn and destroy the other frontier towns."[4] In February and March, the combined Native forces would indeed bring fire, destruction, and terror to eastern New England towns nearly to Boston.

In the meantime, James Quannapohit learned that his life was in danger and had decided to return to the English. The two scouts had invented the plausible story that they had come from Deer Island to discover the condition of "their countrymen" who were fighting the English "so they might be better able to advise their friends at Deer Island and elsewhere, what course to steer for the future."[5] At first this seemed to be accepted, and one of the sachems, Mautampe of Quabaug, told Quannapohit to come with him to Metacom's camp in order to inform the Wampanoag leader about the latest news from Boston and the Narragansetts' involvement in the war. But Hassanamisset's minister, Joseph Tukapawillin, quietly told Quannapohit that Metacom had given instructions to bring him and a few other prominent Christian Indians for torture and death. So far he had been protected by Monoco, also known as One Eyed John, a "great captain" from Nashaway who had fought with James against the Mohawks in 1665, in an attack by Christian Indians supported by Massachusetts. But that protection would not extend beyond the Nipmuc camp, and so James decided to leave quickly.

Lancaster Targeted

On January 24, Quannapohit reported to Gookin what he had witnessed among the Nipmucs and warned him about the planned attack on Lancaster. But the English did little, either because they suspected Quannapohit or were dealing with other threats. On February 1, Nipmucs attacked the garrison of Thomas Eames (at modern Framingham, Massachusetts), killing the family and cattle of the absent trader and burning their house, barn, corn, and hay. This was probably a deliberate feint by the Indians, and indeed Lancaster was left completely unguarded.

Sixteen days later, on February 9, Job Kattenanit returned to Gookin's home with the intelligence that the Narragansetts had joined up with the Nipmucs, and that Monoco had left camp with four hundred warriors and would attack Lancaster the following day. Gookin and a neighbor on the Massachusetts Council ordered garrisons from nearby towns to assist Lancaster, but only the one at Marlborough received word by the morning and was not able to arrive until after the attack. The attackers were well acquainted with the town: they first burned the bridge to bar any rescuers and then torched houses in the town, including the garrison of the village minister, Joseph Rowlandson, who had gone to Boston to seek more soldiers. Several in that garrison were killed, but most who fled the flames were taken prisoner.

One of those captives was Mary Rowlandson. In 1682, she would publish an account of her three months among the Indians, *The Sovereignty and Goodness of God*. Rowlandson's story became a prototype for a huge body of American literature known as the "captivity narrative." Her account of the attack on Lancaster evoked the terror that was such a significant part of King Philip's War, and its imagery and sensibility would find their way into many nineteenth-century novels and twentieth-century films.

Rowlandson began by recalling that the assault began at sunrise, and that shortly after she glimpsed other houses burning theirs was also attacked. "Some in our house were fighting for their lives, others wallowing in their blood, the house on fire over our heads, and the bloody heathen ready to knock us on the head, if we stirred out." But the fire forced them out the door. In the hail of musket balls, her brother-in-law was killed, she was wounded,

Natives Ascendant

and the baby in her arms was shot through the bowels and hand. "Thus were we butchered by those merciless heathen, standing amazed, with the blood running down to our heels." Her oldest sister, still in the house, "seeing those woeful sights, the infidels ha[u]ling mothers one way, and children another, and some wallowing in their blood: and her elder son telling her that her son William was dead, and myself was wounded, she said, And, Lord, let me die with them; which was no sooner said, but she was struck with a bullet, and fell down dead over the threshold."

A group of raiders grabbed Mary. "Come go along with us," they told her. "I told them they would kill me: they answered, If I were willing to go along with them, they would not hurt me." So she went, and the death and destruction at her home and in the village were overwhelming even as she saw "*the works of the Lord*" in those "*desolations*." It was a "solemn sight to see so many Christians lying in their blood, some here, and some there, like a company of sheep torn by wolves. All of them stripped naked by a company of hellhounds, roaring, singing, ranting and insulting, as if they would have torn our very hearts out." This "dolefullest night that ever my eyes saw" left her with a palatable hatred of Indians. "Oh, the roaring, and singing and dancing, and yelling of those black creatures in the night, which made the place a lively resemblance of hell. And as miserable was the waste that was there made, of Horses, Cattle, Sheep, Swine, Calves, Lambs, roasting Pigs, and Fowls (which they had plundered in the Town) some roasting, some lying and burning, and some boyling to feed our merciless Enemies."[6]

The Native attack on Lancaster was for them a successful opening to what became a long winter offensive. The Nipmucs, Narragansetts, and Wampanoags had joined forces in a devastating attack. Suffering few if any losses, the warriors destroyed the village, killed nearly fourteen, obtained needed provisions, and captured over twenty of the colonists. Eastern Woodland peoples traditionally sought captives for adoption to replace deceased clan members or for torture to continue the contest with the enemy and purge anger from the community. But the Lancaster colonists were taken for other reasons.

Initially the captives served as markers of high status for the households who adopted or "owned" them. Rowlandson was taken with others to Wachusett, where she was purchased from Monoco by the Narragansett sachem Quinnapin. Because she was submissive and useful to Quinnapin and other warriors (including Metacom!) as a seamstress, she ended up having good relations with many of the men. But Rowlandson was abused by Weetamoo, the

Pocasset "squaw sachem" and Quinnapin's spouse, at least in part because the minister's wife felt required to submit to Indian *men* (in proper English manner) but not to *women*. Later, as the war turned against them, Native leaders would seek to trade captives—Rowlandson in particular—as a token of their good feelings or for favorable terms in ending the war.

Closer to Boston

After returning to Wachusett, at least three hundred warriors led by Monoco headed east, targeting Medfield, a fairly new town just twenty miles from Boston. Unlike Lancaster, Medfield had obtained extra protection, with one hundred local militia reinforced by eighty infantry and twenty cavalry. But the Indians managed to infiltrate the town after midnight on February 21 without being seen. They hid during the night "under the Sides of the Barns and Fences of their Orchards" and began shooting the inhabitants and burning their houses as they emerged in the morning.[7]

The results were effective for the attackers, who surprised and overwhelmed the defenders. But the experience was particularly horrific for the townspeople who were targets. Thomas Thurston's wife fled her lodgings at a friend's house when the attack began; she was hit or fell and appeared dead to the Indians, so "they stript her [naked] & tooke of[f] her head cloths." She regained consciousness, grabbed a blanket as cover, and ran to a neighbor's house—but her bloody, naked appearance was such "a frightfull spectacle" that they did not recognize her.[8]

The Indians destroyed Medfield, killing about twenty people and taking large numbers captive. As the raiders left and set fire to the two bridges crossing the Charles River, one of them (legend names James the Printer, the Nipmuc who had helped print Eliot's Bibles at Harvard College) left a note "that the Indians that thou hast provoked to Wrath and Anger" would if necessary wage twenty more years of war, and noting that his people "had nothing to lose, whereas [settlers] had Houses, Barnes, and Corn."[9] Four days later, a raiding party burned seven or eight buildings in Weymouth along the coast just south of Boston. Colonists throughout the region, even in Boston, feared that the merciless "savages" would suddenly appear at any moment and begin slaughtering "civilized" women and children.

About thirty miles west of Boston, Groton was hit several times in early March. The town with sixty families was seemingly prepared: it had five garrisons, four along Main Street built so each could cover the other. On March 2, a band raided eight or nine houses, stealing cattle without killing any inhabitants. A week later, several warriors spent two days looting homes in the town and then ambushed a group of hay harvesters, killing one and taking another captive for later torture (although he managed to escape). Finally, on the thirteenth, the Indians made a full-scale attack on the town.

As with Medfield, warriors infiltrated Groton at night. In the morning, Monoco had two men show themselves on a hillside to draw out soldiers from a garrison; part of his forces then ambushed the soldiers as they reached the top of the hill, while another part assaulted and occupied the largely undefended house—allowing the women and children to escape to a neighboring garrison. The attackers took food from and burned the abandoned houses, and they tried another feint to draw out soldiers and make another garrison vulnerable, but without success. At that point, some left the town, while others, including Monoco, actually spent the night in the garrison.

That evening, Monoco engaged in a shouted conversation with "*his old Neighbor*" Captain James Parker, urging peace while "mixing bitter Sarcasms, with several blasphemous Scoffs and Taunts" at Christianity, and boasting that he "would burn that Town of *Groton*, and the next time he would burn *Chelmsford, Concord, Watertown, Cambridge, Charlestown, Roxbury, and Boston.*"[10] In the morning, the town had indeed been mostly reduced to ashes and was abandoned. Several days later, Indian forces burned all of Warwick, Rhode Island, except for one stone house, although they killed only one settler as the town had been largely abandoned.

For the colonists, a particularly disturbing assault came on March 12, when warriors attacked William Clark's garrison on the Eel River two miles south of Plymouth, killing Clark, his wife, and their nine children. Increase Mather, Boston minister and one of the most prominent men in New England, wrote that Clark's wife was "the Daughter of a godly Father and Mother that came to *New England* on the account of Religion, and she herself also a pious and prudent Woman." The leader of the attack "was one *Totoson*, a fellow who was well acquainted with that house, and had received many kindnesses there, it being the manner of those bruitish men, who are only skilful to destroy, to deal worst with those who have done most for them."[11]

The attacks in March highlighted how religious aspects of the war were important to both sides. Mather wrote angrily that the Nipmucs who attacked Groton on the thirteenth burned first "the *House of God*," and then went to the Reverend Willard's garrison house and "scoffed and blasphemed . . . and tauntingly, said, *What will you do for a house to pray in now we have burnt your Meeting-house?* Thus hath the Enemy done wickedly in the Sanctuary, they have burnt up the Synagogues of God in the Land; they have cast fire into the Sanctuary; they have cast down the dwelling place of his name to the Ground."[12] Such episodes, along with the attacks on towns that targeted families, outraged colonial authorities to the point that they felt justified in giving captured Indians no quarter.

In the West

In the meantime, the United Colonies on February 8 had decided to raise an army of six hundred troops commanded by Major Thomas Savage, half from Massachusetts and half from Connecticut, to meet at Brookfield at the end of the month. Six Native scouts, including Job Kattenanit and James Quannapohit, joined the Massachusetts forces, and a company of Mohegans and Pequots went with Robert Treat's Connecticut troops. After the army assembled at Brookfield, Savage received information from an English girl who had escaped from the Nipmucs that they were staying in villages to the north and west. But when the expedition reached the Quabaug (Miller's) River, they found that the Indians had already crossed, and Savage decided not to risk following, particularly since his supplies were low. This was the point at which, as Rowlandson later wrote, "the Indians derided the slowness, and dullness of the English army."[13] Savage instead took his force to Hadley in order to forestall attacks on the extremely vulnerable English settlements in the Connecticut Valley. Indeed, on March 14, a sizeable group of warriors assaulted Northampton, broke through the outside palisade in three places, killed six people, and burned four or five houses. But after this initial surprise, the soldiers led by Treat and William Turner managed to drive off the attackers.

Nearly two weeks later, on March 26, a small band ambushed a small party at Longmeadow heading for church; while the colonists had a military escort, the relative peace in the area made the party complacent, and the warriors were able to pick off those at the rear of the column. Two were killed immediately. After the soldiers raced into town and dropped off the women riding with them, they returned and began searching for two women and two children thrown by their horses and captured by the Natives. Hubbard wrote that when they confronted the Indians and their captives, "the cruel Wretches endeavored to have killed them all, but in Haste only wounded them with their Hatchets, yet so as one of the poor Creatures recovered; the other with the Children dyed of their Wounds." But contrary to Nathaniel Saltonstall's slander that "the Heathen . . . first forced [women captives] to satisfie their filthy Lusts," which became an Anglo-American stereotype, the two "did not complain of any Incivility toward them" during captivity, and Mary Rowlandson and other captives reported similar respectful treatment.[14]

Rowlandson herself became essentially a domestic within the Indian camp, even as she perceived the Natives more as instruments of God's will than human beings. "Although I had met with so much affliction, and my heart was many times ready to break, yet could I not shed one tear in their sight: but rather had been all this while in a maze, and like one astonished: but now I may say as, Psalm 137.1. *By the rivers of Babylon, there we sat down: yea, we wept when we remembered Zion.*" She cooked and sewed for her household and others, at one point even spending time with Metacom, who "bade me come in and sit down, and asked me whether I would smoke," but she refused even though she had taken tobacco before the war; now she saw it as the devil's temptation "to make men lose their precious time." Metacom asked her to make a shirt for his son; in return, he gave her a shilling, which her master allowed her to keep and with which she bought some horsemeat to try to relieve her hunger.

Other than the attack on Northampton and the Longmeadow ambush, the Connecticut River valley was fairly peaceful during the winter and early spring: the English stayed in their few fortified towns, and Natives went to secluded villages to plant and replenish supplies.

Attacks on Marlborough, Providence, and Other Towns

Back east, Nipmucs, Narragansetts, and allied warriors continued to launch devastating attacks that drove many refugees into Boston and made the colonists alarmed that the capitol town would be next and that no place was safe. They seemed to have no defense against the ability of warriors to enter towns without notice and then attack at dawn's light. The attackers appeared to make no distinction between soldiers and civilians, men and women, young and old, but targeted all of the settlers and their homes, and (for good reason) the English seemed to particularly fear the pain of being clubbed or burned to death—which is how many had died so far in the war—and the humiliation of being scalped.

Colonists began to see and fear Indians everywhere, sounding alarms when they thought they heard noises or saw movement in the woods. Towns all over the region quickly erected palisades and fortified garrisons. The resulting drain on resources, social conflicts, and paranoia handicapped their defense. After Indians were reported by Andover and Haverhill residents in the north, Massachusetts moved troops into those towns. But instead, on March 26, about three hundred Native men assaulted Marlborough and burned most of the town; the inhabitants fled, although soldiers continued to garrison the few remaining houses. On the same day, a small Native force burned the abandoned village of Simsbury, Connecticut. And also on March 26, at least three hundred Narragansetts encountered and decimated a Plymouth company that had entered Rhode Island to search for the enemy along the Pawtucket River just five miles north of Providence. Of the eighty-three men in the company, twenty were Wampanoags from Cape Cod; fifty-five of the English (including their commander, Captain Michael Pierce of Scituate) and ten of "their Indian Friends" were killed.[15] Two days later, Canonchet's band attacked Rehoboth, burning barns, homes, and mills. The following day, March 29, the same band laid waste to Providence—but Canonchet and other warriors first met with his friend Roger Williams.

A strange theological and political debate ensued between Williams and the Narragansetts as Providence burned in the background. Williams asked "Why they assaulted us With burning and Killing who ever were Neighbours to them (and looking back) said I this Hous[e] of mine now burning before mine Eyes hath Lodged kindly Some Thousands of You these Ten Years." They replied that Rhode Island had joined forces with Massachusetts and Plymouth. Williams told them that his colony had behaved peaceably, but that they were "like Wolves tearing, and Devouring the Innocent." The Indians "Confessed they were in A Strange Way. 2ly we had forced them to it. 3ly that God was [with] them and Had forsaken us for they had so prospered in Killing and Burning us far beyond What we did against them." Williams bitterly taunted them that they were wrong, for "God had prospered us so that wee had driven the Wampanoogs with Phillip out of his Countrie and the Nahigonsiks out of their Countre, and had destroyed Multitudes of them in Fighting and Flying, In Hungr and Cold etc.: and that God would help us to Consume them." Yet even after Williams again met and upbraided the attackers, they parted with surprising amity. He noted that that "they were so Civill that they called after me and bid me not go near the Burned Houses for their might be Indians [that] might mischief me, but goe by the Water Side."[16]

The terrible, devastating attacks spread throughout eastern Massachusetts. By the first week in April, the large Indian force, as Hubbard put it, "began to scatter about in small Parties, doing what Mischief they could about the *Massachusetts*, killing a Man at *Weymouth*, another at *Hingham*, as they lay skulking up and down in Swamps and Holes"—the English still had problems dealing with the wetlands and woods that lay around nearly every town—"to assault any that occasionally looked never so little into the Woods; sometimes alarming the Towns about Boston by discharging Guns upon particular Persons; at *Billerica*, *Braintree*, and at *[W]rentham*."[17] There are hints in other town records of alarms if not raids otherwise unreported. In response, Savage withdrew most Massachusetts troops from the valley towns and went east to confront the growing threat.

On April 9, warriors attacked Bridgewater, near Swansea, burning a house and a barn and destroying food stores. Six days later, a band burned abandoned Chelmsford; two days after that, a different group destroyed the buildings that remained in Marlborough. Swiftly moving warriors killed settlers and burned buildings in Andover, Hingham, Haverhill, Hadley, Worcester, Mendon, and Woburn. The English tried to hit back: the day after Marlborough was burned, a band of militia from Sudbury found the Native camp near the devastated town and shot from concealed positions, wounding about thirty. But most of the time the colonial soldiers found themselves under siege, overwhelmed (as with the Plymouth militia), and unable to respond effectively.[18]

Many in England were concerned about how their American cousins were faring in the war. In early 1676, Massachusetts magistrate Nathaniel Saltonstall published in London a *Brief Account* that emphasized how few houses were "left standing" in each town hit by Indian attack and mourned that more than eight hundred English of all ages had been killed. Worse was how "the Heathen" treated their victims: "Many have been destroyed with exquisite Torments and most inhumane barbarities . . . if they were Women, they first forced them to satisfie their filthy lusts, and then murthered them, either cutting off the head, ripping open the Belly, or skulping the head of skin and hair, and hanging them up as Trophees; wearing mens fingers as bracelets about their Necks, and stripes of their skins which they dresse for Belts."

Saltonstall also focused on how these "brute and savage beasts" had treated English cattle: they killed and ate few, "but rather cut their bellies, and letting them go severall days, trailing their guts after them, putting out their eyes, or cutting off one leg, &c."[19] While his lascivious description of warriors raping women was pure propaganda—there were no reports of rape—his account is very accurate in showing how the Natives targeted cattle as symbols of the unwelcome changes that the English brought to their region.

Colonial Crises

In the two decades before the war erupted, religious conflicts and political tensions seemed to multiply in southern New England, particularly in Massachusetts. Towns jealously guarded their interests and quarreled with each other over land claims. Quakers and Anabaptists challenged colonial leaders. The Restoration of Charles II to the English throne in 1660 had been a distinct calamity, particularly with the arrival in 1664 of a royal commission that depicted the colony as one in which a minority of fanatical nonconformists forced their rule on the majority and recommended that the Crown reduce its autonomy, recognize Native sovereignty, and grant rights of worship to dissidents. The Puritans had dodged that threat, but the divisions and anxieties in Massachusetts and the other colonies deepened as the Indian attacks intensified.

Many worried that God might be using the Indians to chastise His wayward people for their sins. On June 22, 1675, Plymouth called a fast day to be held two days later to seek pardon "for all those sins whereby we have provoked our good God" (including materialism and religious toleration) and to obtain his support in "subduing the heathen"—and that turned out to be the day the war began. As the war went bad for the colonists, ministers discovered additional sins in their midst that might be causing God to smite them through the victorious heathen. In October and November, as English military disasters multiplied, the Massachusetts General Court called for the reformation of fourteen kinds of sins committed by their people, including swearing, idleness, oppressively high prices, illegal trading, men sporting long hair, and other ills "especially amongst the young."[20]

These anxieties were widely shared among the colonists. Mary Rowlandson later wrote that she could "but admire to see the wonderful providence of God in preserving the heathen for further affliction to our poor country."

Many times she saw them eat what "a hog or dog would hardly touch" and then go on "to be scourge to His people." Rowlandson and many other Puritans felt that the war was due not to conflicts over land and power, but because "our perverse and evil carriages in the sight of the Lord, have so offended Him, that instead of turning His hand against [the Indians], the Lord feeds and nourishes them up to be a scourge to the whole Land."[21]

While history tends to depict this war as English against Indians, different interests and perceptions generated internal conflicts among the colonists and their governments. Settlers in outlying towns, only recently created and now prime targets, resisted Boston's efforts to conscript soldiers, tax for the war, or garrison troops at the town's expense. John Bishop of Massachusetts told Increase Mather that his neighbors found it "difficult, dissatisfying, & uncomfortable . . . to send out their children, & other dear relations unto the war."[22] By February 1676, some towns in Massachusetts reported that nearly 50 percent of those called to service refused to appear. Others deserted after joining. Townspeople in Billerica, Chelmsford, Reading, and other places refused to prosecute this evasion of military service and ignored seditious speech against the war and regional elites. Local companies acted contrary to policy and in ways that seemed as "savage" as the Indians; for example, Mosely's company on several occasions arrested Christian Indians without a warrant, torturing one and threatening to lynch others, and some Chelmsford militia murdered the few remaining Pennacook allies at Wamesit and burned their homes.

There were also strong tensions between the colonies. Before the war began, Massachusetts authorities had told its smaller neighbor not to press Metacom so hard, and Rhode Island deputy governor John Easton showed considerable sympathy for the Wampanoag sachem's charges against the neighboring colony. Months after the shooting started, Bishop told Mather that he knew many who wondered "whether our English were wholly innocent" in this conflict, indeed that Plymouth's "dishonorable" actions might have caused the war.[23] Massachusetts had long hoped to eliminate Rhode Island, which it viewed as a refuge of dissenters and troublemakers, and many in the smaller colony feared that efforts by the United Colonies against the Narragansetts were directed as much at them. Connecticut was reluctant to ask neighboring New York for assistance because that royal colony claimed territory between the Connecticut River and the Hudson; indeed, in July 1675, at the outbreak of the war, Governor Sir Edmund Andros dispatched a small armed force to try to seize Saybrook at the mouth of the Connecticut. While the United Colonies was supposed to coordinate war policy, each colony pursued divergent interests. For example, on May 1, 1676, Connecticut tried once again to extend its authority up the Connecticut River into Massachusetts by offering peace to the Wabanakis at Squakeag if they agreed to live on reserves (like the Pequots) near Hartford and warned the settlers at Hadley against attacking the Indians during the period of truce.

As the colonists suffered more losses, their suspicions grew that the hostile Indians must have some help from inside the colonial community, and they began to turn on those sympathetic to the Natives. In late August 1675, John Eliot and Daniel Gookin argued "daily" against the initial guilty verdicts and death sentences for the Christian Indians from Marlborough accused of attacking Lancaster. Their efforts were successful, although condemned by some magistrates as "Impertinences and multitudinous"; Massachusetts Council member John Oliver told Gookin that he should "be confined among his Indians" instead of serving as a justice of the peace. On the other hand, when a crowd several nights later visited Oliver and asked him to "break open the Prison, and take one Indian out thence and Hang him," the captain "took his Cane and cudgeled them stoutly."[24]

Later that winter, Eliot and Gookin were threatened with death by Bostonians as they sought to supply the Indians on Deer Island with food. Even John Pynchon, one of the most powerful men in the colony, was not free from suspicion. Residents of Springfield (most of which he owned), hearing that an Indian man in town might have taken part in recent attacks, called for his death. Pynchon sent him to the English forces for protection, whereupon Pynchon became the target of the crowd's anger.

Ironically, whereas leaders of Plymouth and Massachusetts listed toleration of Anabaptists and Quakers among their communal sins, those dissidents were happy to point out that the Indians' successes were God's justice for past and present persecutions by the Puritans. Quaker pacifists refused to bear arms, called for peace, and (in the eyes of Puritan leaders) refused to give proper respect and obedience to those anointed with power. Those in Rhode Island sometimes protested the violations of their territory by troops of the United Colonies; Easton complained that the Puritans had launched the December campaign against the Narragansetts without getting the permission of the Crown or his colony.

These protests and others were sent to England, where they were read along with the narratives by Saltonstall, Hubbard, and others supporting the Puritans and railing against the Indians. Many accounts were published on both sides of the Atlantic, in addition to unpublished letters and other materials sent to England. In fact, within England the war was better publicized than any previous event in American history. Most of these accounts were weighted against the Puritans. The *London Gazette*, which regularly reported on the war, published as supplements about six detailed pamphlets that provided extensive details of particular events; five of these were sympathetic to Metacom and quite critical of New England's leaders, particularly those in Boston. Knowledge of the war and criticism of Boston's Puritan leadership were so widespread that Virginia governor William Berkeley and others used the Bay Colony's problems to emphasize their own loyalty to the Crown.

As a result of the accounts from the colonies and the overwhelming wave of English criticism, royal authorities began (again) reviewing the actions of Massachusetts with an eye toward curbing or ending that colony's autonomy—which would serve as an example to Connecticut and Plymouth. New England authorities were aware of this threat, and for that very reason they were reluctant to ask England for assistance. The 1664 royal commission had been particularly critical that the Puritans had created the United Colonies without the permission of Crown or Parliament, and of course that was the organization that was coordinating the military efforts. But finally, in early April, the Massachusetts Council formally submitted to the Crown information about the war and a request for *monetary* assistance. Royal authorities made no immediate response.

The Battle of Sudbury

On April 21, the largest fight of the war came to Sudbury, just seventeen miles west of Boston. We know from Rowlandson's story that the five hundred warriors led by Muttawmp came directly from the large camp at Mount Wachusett. Her *Narrative* also provides the only eyewitness of a divination ceremony by New England Indians, before the warriors left to attack Sudbury. The warriors gathered in a circle around two men on a deer skin who were apparently *pawwaws*—men known for their ability to understand or manipulate the supernatural—and began "striking upon the ground with their hands, and with sticks, and muttering or humming with their mouths."

With the background of drumming and humming, one of the pawwaws

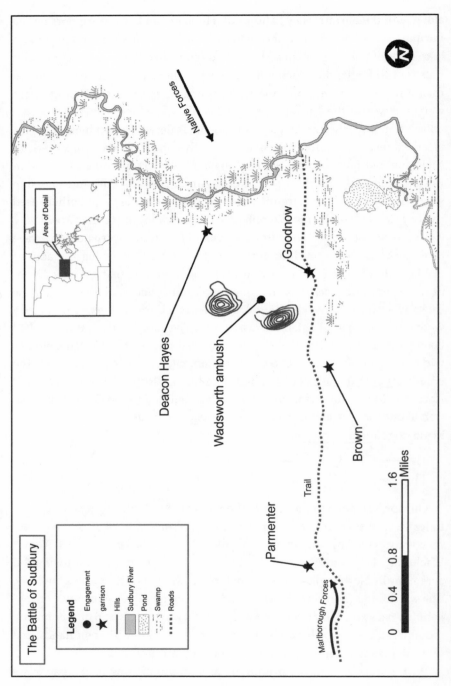

The Battle of Sudbury

"made a speech" to which the warriors answered, in a call-and-response pattern that continued "many times together." The other pawwaw held a gun and began a ritual in which he started to leave the deer skin, was called back by the warriors, started to leave again, but was once again called back. Their tempo and fervor increased; the pawwaw with the gun was given a second one to hold and continued to go back and forth as the other man chanted and the warriors responded. Finally, he stopped outside the circle and, as the warriors beat and sang, "stood reeling and wavering . . . Then they called him with exceeding great vehemency, all of them, one and another. After a little while he turned in, staggering as he went, with his arms stretched out, in either hand a gun. As soon as he came in they all sang and rejoiced exceedingly a while."[25]

The attackers followed the same strategy as in Medfield: on the east side of the Sudbury River, they infiltrated the village during the night of April 20. That very evening, Captain Samuel Wadsworth of Milton had marched through Sudbury with about seventy men on the way to Marlborough. The next morning, the warriors emerged and began burning abandoned houses and besieging garrisons. A group also surrounded and poured gunfire into the Deacon Hayes garrison on the western side of the river. Word of the fight reached the nearby town of Concord, and eleven men headed downriver to help; all but one were killed as they reached Sudbury meadow directly in front of the Hayes garrison. Troops arrived from Watertown and managed to push the attackers from the village to the western side of the river, but they came close to getting surrounded and so retreated to the Goodnow garrison about one-third of a mile south of the Hayes garrison. Wadsworth brought fifty men east from Marlborough as the battle raged, but they ran into an ambush in a pass between Goodman Hill and Green Hill. They formed a square and managed to fight for four hours while losing only five men, but as night fell the Indians set fire to Green Hill, forcing the English to retreat and lose their defensive position; about thirty men (including Wadsworth) were killed.

The Native forces (which may have included Metacom) performed in ways unlike the stereotype of the "skulking savage." They slugged it out all day with the English, kept the troops in the Hayes garrison bottled up, shifted positions and tactics to trap and decimate attacking forces, burned the abandoned houses, and besieged the garrisons. As they passed through Marlborough on the way home, they shouted seventy-four times to show the surviving troops in the garrison how many Englishmen they thought they had killed back in Sudbury.

But the Indians were unhappy with the results of the battle, probably because, contrary to the prediction of the pawwaw, they had not taken any of the garrisons. Rowlandson later noted that the warriors returned to the camp at Mount Wachusett "without that rejoicing and triumphing over their victory, which they were wont to show at other times, but rather like dogs (as they say) which have lost their ears." She was surprised at their dejected faces, since they had lost only five or six men. When they left for Sudbury, she noted, "they acted as if the devil had told them that they should gain the victory," but now it seemed that "the devil had told them they should have a fall." And indeed, she wrote, "quickly they began to fall," and toward summer time "they came to utter ruin."[26]

Turning Points

The beginning of the end for Metacom's uprising was Mohawk intervention on behalf of the colonists. The tribe's actions open a window into the larger world of northeastern trade and military alliances. The Iroquois Confederation had for decades sought direct access to the European fur trade, in the 1640s opening a series of vicious "beaver wars" with the Hurons to the west, who were connected to New France, and the Mahicans to the east along the Hudson River, who were connected with New Amsterdam. The Mohawks, keepers of the Iroquois "eastern door," were successful in driving the Mahicans across the Hudson while developing a trading relationship with the Dutch. When England and James Duke of York took control of that colony in 1664, the Iroquois and Governor Andros both saw opportunities in an alliance.

At the outbreak of the war, some Mohawks were willing to give the Wampanoags guns for wampum. But Metacom also needed allies, and in December he went west to Schaghticoke in the Hudson River valley, north of Albany, in an effort to seek the support of the Mahicans and Mohawks against the English. While the Mohawks had in the past raided southern New England Native communities, Metacom hoped that at this point they would share his dislike of English expansion. But the Mohawks had already received a message from Governor Andros seeking to strengthen his alliance with that tribe and asking them to attack Metacom as a personal favor. This agreement forged the

THE DESTRUCTION OF SUDBURY.

Indian Attack on Sudbury, April 21, 1676. Illustration in "Adventures of the Early Settlers of New England," *Harper's Weekly* (June 1857), 35. Courtesy Library of Congress.

famous Covenant Chain, which quickly became the foremost diplomatic and military alliance in the northeast and operated according to Iroquois protocols even as more English colonies became links in it.

The Mohawks were happy to create this new alliance by assailing their ancient enemies, and in February they attacked and decimated the Wampanoags traveling near Schaghticoke. The details of the battle are unknown, but it was probably a deadly surprise. Most of Metacom's men were killed, and the survivors fled east. The sachem arrived back at Mount Wachusett by February, where he met Mary Rowlandson (and asked her to sew a shirt for his son), and no doubt angered the Nipmuc and Narragansett war leaders with the bad news that so many of the Wampanoag warriors were dead. Those leaders must have become even angrier when they found out in the spring that the dreaded Mohawks were sending war parties into Massachusetts, perhaps following up on their February victory, or responding to Connecticut's effort in April to "engage ye Mowhawkes against our Indian enemies."[27] By early May, Increase Mather noted, Boston received word from Connecticut that "God had let loose the Mohawks upon our Enemies."[28]

The second critical turning point was the capture and death of the powerful war leader Canonchet. As March ended, Captain George Denison and James Avery of Stonington, Connecticut, led a force into western Rhode Island to find and destroy Narragansetts in the area. The forty-seven Englishmen in the band were noticeably outnumbered by eighty Indians: twenty Niantics led by Catapazat, Pequots led by Cassannamon, and Mohegans led by Oweneco, eldest son of Uncas. These Natives would play a critical role in the campaign that would shift the dynamics of the war. On April 3, five days after the destruction of Providence, the patrol encountered and killed "a stout Indian of the Enemies," and they took captive two elderly women who told them that the Narragansett sachem was nearby, "which welcom [sic] News put new Life into the wearied Soldiers, that had travelled hard many Days, and met with no Booty till now."[29] The Indian scouts confirmed the intelligence and guided the company to a bluff or hill overlooking a cluster of wigwams along the Blackstone River in the area of Pawtucket, Rhode Island.

Canonchet was in one of the wigwams, with just seven of his men. He sent two up to the top of the hill to keep watch, but they were startled by the approach of Denison's company and ran back and past the wigwams without giving an alarm. The Narragansett sachem sent another man to see what was up; when he also fled, he dispatched two more to the hilltop, and finally when those two ran away one "either indued [imbued] with more Courage, or a better sense of his Duty, informed him in great haste that all the English Army was upon him." With only three warriors left by his side, Canonchet knew he had no chance to resist and so "began to Dodg[e] with his Pursuers, running round the Hill on the contrary Side" in an effort to escape.

The Niantics guessed that the fleeing warrior was a Narragansett and with a few fast Englishmen ran after him. As one of the Niantics closed the distance rapidly, the sachem "cast off first his Blanket, then his Silver-lac'd Coat" (received at the October 1675 Boston conference) and a large "Belt of Peag" (wampum) in a futile effort to run faster. And when Canonchet tried to dash through the Blackstone River, he slipped on a rock and fell into the water, soaking his gun. Although he was able to quickly get back on his feet, the accident disheartened him "so as he became like a rotten Stick, void of Strength" and allowed the smaller Niantic to capture him about a hundred yards on the other side of the river.[30]

Denison's men held a hearing, telling Canonchet of "his Breach of Faith, and how he boasted he would not deliver up a Wampanoog, or the paring of a *Wampanoogs* Nail; that he would burn the English alive in their Houses; to which he replyed, others were as forward for the War as himself, and that he desired to hear no more thereof. And when he was told his Sentence was to dye, he said, he liked it well, that he should dye before his Heart was soft, or had spoken any thing unworthy of himself." He refused their offer of clemency if he would send "an old Counsellor" urging those at Wachusett to surrender to the English.[31] Then they took him to Stonington, where he was shot by Oweneco (as Uncas three decades before had executed Canonchet's father Miantonomi) and two Pequots. The colonists viewed the sachem as a traitor who had shown "Pride and Insolency," as they cut off his head and sent it to Hartford.[32]

Another version of Canonchet's death is that the sachem told his captors that "he wisht rather to die" at Oweneco's hands than rot in prison, and "had 2,000 Men [who] would revenge his Death." At Stonington, "that all might share in the Glory of destroying so great a Prince . . . the Pequods shot him, the Mohegins cut off his Head and quartered his Body, and the Ninnicrofts [Ninigret's] Men made the Fire and burned his Quarters; and as a Token of their Love and Fidelity to the English, presented his Head to the Council at Hartford."[33] Before Canonchet was executed, according to Hubbard, he told the colonists "that the killing him would not end the War; but it was a considerable Step thereunto." Indeed, although the Puritans continued to experience tribulations—more attacks, economic hardships, religious and social discord, the threat of intervention by the Crown—the war in southern New England soon turned in favor of the English.[34]

Indian Declension

In the wake of Canonchet's death and the alarming intrusions of Mohawks, divisions between tribal sachems and between different generations among those camped at Wachusett widened. Given that the Iroquois were already greatly feared and generally subjected their captives to slow, agonizing torture, fleeing or attempting peace talks with the English probably seemed better than facing Mohawk attacks. By mid-April the older sachems began negotiating with Boston authorities, exchanging captives for a ransom and the possibility of peace. Some even threatened to turn Metacom over to the English.

Hunger was also a growing threat. The harsh winter had created food shortages for everyone in the region, but particularly for the Natives who could not get to stored supplies or their fields in the early spring. James Quannapohit had reported to Boston at the end of January that the Nipmucs were dependent on venison along with a few supplies taken from abandoned villages, and when that was gone "they wilbe in want of corne" but hoped (and needed) to obtain more corn from their raid on Lancaster.[35] Mary Rowlandson provided a vivid description of the hunger that she shared with her enemies during her captivity at Wachusett and Squakeag and wrote with scorn of the horse hooves, maggots, bark, and other things that they were forced to eat.

The need for food showed in the way that, in every raid, warriors not only killed and gutted cows and sheep but (as in the Warwick attack) were beginning to take "a considerable Booty of Cattel."[36] Yet these attacks netted insufficient meat—or perhaps many spurned eating cattle as unmanly or contrary to the right way for warriors—and little grain. Canonchet had remained in Narragansett after the attack on Providence in order to obtain his tribe's seed corn and take it to Squakeag, an effort that led to his capture. Lack of food was one more reason that the Native alliance splintered in May, and Narragansetts and Wampanoags returned to their home territories, where they became vulnerable to colonial patrols. Disease accompanied malnutrition: according to James Printer, the literate Christian Nipmuc, more warriors died from disease than from the English musket balls.

The Indians, like the English, faced internal conflicts, and not surprisingly the tensions between and within tribes seemed to grow as conditions worsened. The Nipmucs were never a coherent polity and clearly had different interests in June 1675: some threw themselves into the war against the English, while others tried to remain neutral, and still others sought to help their Christian allies. Most of those at Hassanamisset who went along with the demands of their cousins in November were still there when Quannapohit arrived a month later; he found that some had joined the war effort while others (like the minister) sought to help the spy in his mission for the English. The Narragansetts had been forced into the war, and while some like Quinnapin remained bellicose, many were eager to find a way out of what seemed like a hopeless cause.

A disagreement between the generations was another fault line. In late January, Quannapohit told his colonial friends that the "cheefe men & old men" among the Nipmucs "were inclinable to have peace again with the English," but that the young warriors saw war as preferable to being sold into slavery.[37] In early April, two Christian Indians sent by Boston to negotiate for Mary Rowlandson's release reported that the Natives at Wachusett were divided, with the older Nipmuc sachems particularly anxious to negotiate with the English and reluctant to pursue war, while a few younger war hawks such as Metacom and Quinnapin rejected conciliation. Daniel Gookin felt that it was this dispute that "caused them to fall out and divide" into smaller groups "which was a means under God to weaken and destroy them."[38]

Those who were uncertain whether to settle or to fight must have tilted toward negotiations as the tide of the war shifted rapidly. On April 3, they lost one of their most effective war sachems when Canonchet was captured. On May 8, Tispaquin, Metacom's brother-in-law and the sachem of Assawompsett, led about three hundred warriors in an attack on Bridgewater. But when they began to burn houses on the south side of the river, the soldiers in the garrisons who had received a day's warning (as Hubbard wrote) "fell upon them with great Resolution, and beat them off, at the same Instant of Time, the Lord of Hosts also fighting for them from Heaven, by sending a Storm of Thunder and Rain very seasonably, which prevented the Burning of the Houses which were fired."[39] The Natives regrouped and tried again on the other side of the river, but again the colonists were able to drive them away, inflicting many casualties while suffering none.

Natives were even more likely than Puritans to see supernatural forces and transcendent meanings behind natural events, and the juxtaposition of the events at Bridgewater that frustrated the attack and caused the death of many warriors would have seemed to Metacom's allies a divine judgment. True, there were a few more victories. Three days later, Tispaquin's force hit Bridgewater again and finished the job on many outlying buildings (but without killing any English), and on the same day they attacked nearby Halifax and burned eleven homes and five barns. On May 20, they raided Scituate and destroyed nineteen buildings. But these were only passing triumphs, although the Wampanoags must have taken satisfaction that they could still wreak havoc against those who had taken their lands.

To the west at the same time came another major setback for the Indians. Many had moved to farming and fishing sites along the Connecticut River between Pocumtuck (abandoned Deerfield) and Peskeompskut (modern Turner's Falls) to feed their families and recover their strength. The colonists knew that the Natives were there, because on May 12 a band had run off a herd of seventy horses and cattle from Hatfield, and Thomas Reed, one of two men captured in April, managed to escape from Peskeompskut and arrived in Hatfield three days after the raid. He reported that there were only about seventy warriors at Peskeompskut; the rest were probably off seeking food or had left to attack Plymouth. The Indians likely felt secure in their villages because the closest English were twenty miles south in Hatfield, all but a few soldiers were serving in the east, and there were easy escape routes north and west. But Reed's report spurred Captain William Turner (a tailor from Boston who, ironically, had been expelled and later imprisoned by Massachusetts authorities for his Baptist beliefs) to quickly organize 150 mounted militia from Hatfield, Northampton, and Hadley, heading north as the sun set on the eighteenth. As they crossed the Deerfield River, the noise was heard by Native men at a small fishing camp—but the warriors investigated and decided that it had been moose.

At daybreak, the English left their horses a half mile from the falls, crossed Fall River, and marched to the top of a steep hill overlooking Peskeompskut. There were no guards. Turner's men rushed the sleeping village and began firing into the dark wigwams. Nearly two hundred Indians—mostly women, children, and elderly—were shot or drowned as they tried to flee; some managed to get into canoes but were killed in the falls. The colonists burned the village and its food stores, and they threw into the river two forges and lead that the Indians had used to repair their firearms and make musket balls.

Warriors hurried back toward the camp and, along with those who had recovered from the attack, attacked the militia on its way home. The inexperienced English panicked and fled despite Turner's efforts to organize a rear guard. The Indian men hunted and harried the scattered colonists all the way back to southern Deerfield, killing thirty-nine, including Turner. The Indians reorganized their forces and, seeking to renew the war and obtain their revenge, attacked Hatfield on May 30, killing seven, taking cattle, and burning many buildings. But the attack on Peskeompskut was a decisive strike for the English: the Natives had lost their supplies and, from sorrow and fearing further attacks, abandoned the fields and fishing camps.

This success in the west and the improving situation in the east spurred the United Colonies to organize a large, joint offensive throughout the region. Captain Daniel Henchman was sent west from Boston through Nipmuc country via Mount Wachusett, and Major John Talcott drove up the Connecticut River valley with 440 English and Mohegan troops. The two forces would meet in Hadley. Along the way, the colonists surprised and captured or killed about one hundred Indians.

The Connecticut troops reached Hadley first, just in time to defend the town (with the help of a cannon) on June 12 against an assault by as many as seven hundred warriors. Legend has it that as the attackers were about to overwhelm the town, the residents were rallied by the sudden appearance of an elderly man: William Goffe, a member of the court that in 1649 sentenced King Charles I to death, and who with the Restoration of Charles II in 1660 had fled to Puritan Massachusetts and gone into hiding. Discouraged from taking Hadley, the Wabanakis broke off the attack and abandoned the war; most of the survivors moved north to join Wabanaki relations or headed west, out of the reach of the colonists. A force sent out of the town on June 16 to scour the valley found only empty Indian villages.

Colonials Take the Offensive

The Henchman-Talcott campaign demonstrated that, by the end of the spring, the colonists had become better at coordinating military efforts and more confident in their ability to control the pace of the war. Their fortifications proved useful in defense and to gather forces for offense. They also began to make better use of Native men: Massachusetts began recruiting Christian Indians from Deer Island, and all of the colonies became willing to offer amnesty to enemy warriors who agreed to help the English.

The colonists also changed their tactics, perhaps because of their new recruits, and became more effective as they targeted Native food stores and smaller groups. This change became particularly critical as the informal alliance against the colonists dissolved into small bands of warriors, some of whom returned to their tribal territories, either to avoid the Mohawks or because they hoped that the English would not know that they had fought or would offer generous terms of peace. During the summer, joint English-Native patrols commanded by competent colonial officers were critical to tracking and capturing or killing scattered bands in Wampanoag and Narragansett territory.

In the middle of April, the Massachusetts Council finally gave permission to create a company of "friendly" Natives, and Captain Samuel Hunting and Lieutenant James Richardson organized in Cambridge forty Christian Indians recruited from Deer Island. They also had to equip the unit, because the colonists had confiscated the Natives' weapons before sending them to the island prison. They were getting ready on the twenty-first to go to Chelmsford for their first posting, but then word came of the attack on Sudbury and they were immediately dispatched to the town, arriving at night after the battle ended.

The following morning, the company was sent to scout the west side of the river, "having stripped themselves, and painted their faces like to the enemy." But all they found were the bodies of the thirty-five soldiers from Marlborough and four enemy warriors. After reporting this sorrowful sight, the Indian company volunteered to bury the dead. "This service, so faithfully performed by our Christian Indians," noted Gookin, "had the effect to abate much, with many, their former hatred of them," especially among the Sudbury residents who had nine months before taken expensive tools, carts, and other farming implements from Natick. When a ship arrived with more weapons, the company also gained forty more Indians, who often served as scouts and in that capacity captured or killed many "and brought their scalps to their commanders."[40] Gookin estimated that during the summer they killed more than four hundred Natives.

The shift in tactics was exemplified by Plymouth's commissions to Benjamin Church and William Bradford. Before the war, Church had excellent relations with various Wampanoag leaders, had tried to get the colonial forces to move more quickly against Metacom to prevent his escape at the beginning of the war, and, as the war progressed, urged the United Colonies to make more liberal use of Indian scouts and to adopt guerrilla tactics. At the end of February his ideas were rejected, but in mid-May he was given command of two hundred men, two-thirds English and one-third Wampanoag, to hunt down the enemy. Bradford (the son of the first governor of the colony) was similarly given a force of 150 English and 50 Cape Cod Indians; Hubbard noted that, thanks to the Indian scouts, Bradford's force "not only escaped an Ambush laid for them . . . , but slew many of those that laid wait for them, without any Loss to themselves."[41]

Church had a particularly dramatic start: in early June, on his way home, he stumbled across Saconnet warriors who told him that Awashonks "was not fond of maintaining a War with the *English*; and that she had left *Philip*, and did not return to him any more." Church arranged to meet in two days with the sachem, her son Peter, her "chief captain," and others he trusted. The conference was initially tense—while only Awashonks and her counselors met him, a few minutes later many of her warriors surrounded him painted for war, with weapons drawn, and looking "very surly"—but old friendships and shared rum and tobacco allowed the Plymouth captain to begin negotiations.[42]

Awashonks and her counselors told Church that they would become loyal subjects of Plymouth if the colony pledged to spare their lives and their families and not to sell any of them into slavery in the West Indies. He reassured them that the colony would agree to their proposals and praised their return to friendship. The Wampanoags then sought to cement their alliance with Church and submission to Plymouth through their warrior tradition, which they calculated would appeal to the English given the circumstances of the war at that time. Awashonks's captain told Church, "*if you'll please to accept of me and my men, and will head us, we'll fight for you, and will help you to Philips head before Indian Corn be ripe.*"[43] The Wampanoag not only fulfilled that pledge but accurately predicted Metacom's fate.

- Between Nat. Am. in New Eng. and English colonists
- King Philip-Metacom - Indian leader
- Aug 12, 1676 - King Philip hunted down, killed
- War continued until treaty on April 1678
- Ruined Puritan New England economy, towns, pop., etc
- Disease desimated New Eng. Nat. Am.
- King Philip distrusted colonists
- The suspicious death of Metacom's brother led to war
- New Eng. Confed. declared war on Ind. Sep 9, 1675
- Colonists def. at battle of Bloody Brook 1675
- Great Swamp Fight - colonists attacked Narragansett semi-neutral
- 1676 - combined Indian tribes attacked Plymouth Plantation, made it deep into their territory.
- Colonists ultimately won sending many Nat. to reservations
- War ultimately ended with Metacom's death

five Colonists Victorious and Wounded

By EARLY JULY 1676, the war in southern New England had entered its final stage as the colonists were clearly winning. Nipmuc and Narragansett warriors and their families surrendered in growing numbers, drawn by colonial offers of clemency and driven by the relentless and effective attacks, their hunger and deprivation, and the constant threat of Mohawk raids. Many who surrendered agreed to work with their captors to help track down other fugitives. At the end of July, Benjamin Church's mostly Indian force picked up Metacom's trail as the Wampanoag sachem headed back to Mount Hope; two weeks later, after his remnant band was spotted by colonists and then followed by Church's company, the Wampanoag leader was killed by a Christian Indian. At the end of the month, Church, with the help of several Wampanoags, captured Metacom's war chief, Annawan; Plymouth then executed him. As the colonists smelled victory, they became more vindictive. Many Indians were executed and their families sold into slavery in the West Indies. Some Natives decided to leave the region, heading west or north to seek refuge among other tribes.

But as the war died down in the south—in fact, the day before Metacom was killed—it flared up again along the coast of Maine. For almost exactly a year, Wabanaki raiding parties attacked and burned trading posts, garrisons, entire towns, and even fishing boats, forcing the English trespassers to flee for points south, including Salem, where some later became involved in the famous witchcraft trials. The violence was connected to the war in the south because Native refugees brought news and a desire for revenge, but Wabanakis already had their own conflicts with the colonists, and this part of the war was really a continuation of the violence that had erupted the previous year. While a truce was reached in August 1677 and formalized eight months later, some developments would shape future wars in the region. Colonial claims of fishing and land rights would continue to spark Wabanaki outrage. English settlers fled the region only to return when peace was restored; the Wabanakis would follow a similar course in later wars. English trader and militia commander Richard Waldron earned Native enmity for two major instances of deceit and betrayal; a decade later he would pay for his deception by being tortured to death.

In addition to the many dead and the devastated communities, the war reshaped politics and social patterns in southern New England. The losers were executed, sold into slavery, fled the region, or found somewhere to hide. The Christian Natives who fought for the English sought to reestablish "praying towns" but for years faced nervous colonists and the continued threat of Mohawk raids. Those who had remained out of the war's maelstrom experienced fewer disruptions. But during the subsequent century, all Indians in the region lost much of their land and deepened their ties to the Anglo-American economy and culture; they became whalers, domestic servants, and laborers, and the men went to fight for the colonists, often against Wabanakis in Maine. In most communities the church (with Indian ministers) gained significance. The colonists also had many of their villages shattered and were debilitated by the war; eastern Massachusetts was particularly hard-hit. They feared continued Indian attacks and so did not reestablish settlements in the middle part of the region or to the north until the Treaty of Utrecht in 1713 ended that threat. Ten to twenty years after the war, the colonists lost to the Crown their claims to sovereignty and power, which for a few years put into danger the very existence of many towns, particularly in Massachusetts. Finally, in the ultimate irony, Plymouth was stripped of its separate existence and annexed to Massachusetts.

The Last Campaign

As the force at Mount Wachusett dissolved and Metacom's allies fled or began to seek peace, the colonies began to think of winning rather than surviving. On June 19, Massachusetts declared that they would show mercy to Indians who surrendered within fourteen days, although the colony's subsequent
actions showed that often meant a quick trial and execution or enslavement
in the Indies instead of immediate death, rather than clemency. At the end of
the month, Connecticut sent John Talcott's force to pursue the Nipmuc and
Narragansett remnants into northern Rhode Island. Connecticut militia from
the eastern towns also made forays into Nipmuc and Narragansett territory.
There is no record of where they attacked or of how many Indians they killed
or drove out of the area.

This last campaign was quite vicious and one-sided. United Colonies commanders could consider any Indians who had not surrendered to Boston as enemy combatants, and those who had sought refuge in Rhode Island were particular targets, in part because the Puritans considered that colony illegitimate
and claimed sections of its territory. On July 2, Talcott attacked a large Narragansett village along a swamp at Nacheck on the Pawtuxet River; the camp
held few warriors, and when the smoke cleared three hours later, the attackers had killed 34 men and 137 women and children, including Ninigret's sister
Quaiapen. Only 45 women and children survived, probably because the Mohegans persuaded Talcott to let them live in order to bring them into the tribe.

A few days earlier, about eighty Narragansetts came near Providence,
whose inhabitants were trying to rebuild their homes and community. Their
sachem Potuck came into the town and asked for help getting safely to Boston
in order to make peace with the English. Several Providence men persuaded
him to go instead to Newport to negotiate terms and to have his people head
for Warwick Neck, along Narragansett Bay about halfway to Newport, where
he could meet them later. Unfortunately, Warwick was just south of the Pawtuxet River. The morning after Talcott decimated the Narragansetts at Nacheck, he heard that Potuck's band was situated on the way back to Mohegan,
and that afternoon without difficulty his force located and "slaughtered"
sixty-seven of them. Rhode Island leaders condemned Talcott's violation of
their decree that United Colonies forces stay out of their territory—since the
colony had not been allowed to be part of the regional organization—but by
then the killing was complete.[1]

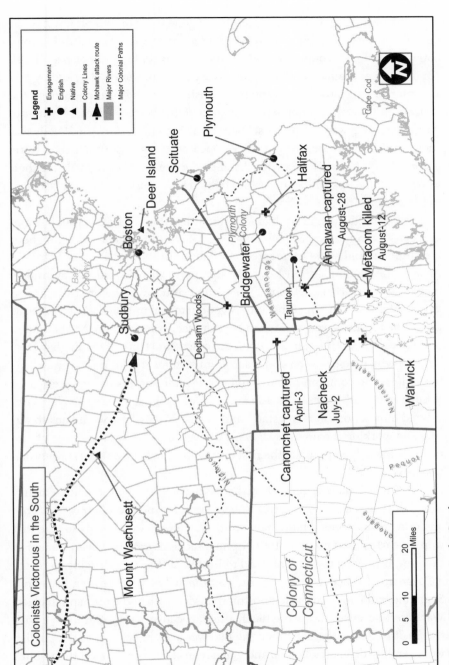

Legend

Engagement		
✚	English	●
Native	▲	

Mohawk attack route
Colony Lines
Major Rivers
Major Colonial Paths

N

Cape Cod

Plymouth

Scituate

Deer Island

Halifax

Boston

Annawan captured
August-28

Bridgewater

Metacom killed
August-12

Sudbury

Plymouth Colony

Wampanoags

Taunton

Dedham Woods

Canonchet captured
April-3

Nacheck
July-2

Warwick

Narragansetts

Mount Wachusett

Nipmucs

Bay Colony

Colonists Victorious in the South

Colony of Connecticut

Pequot

Mohegans

0   5   10   20
Miles

Colonists Victorious in the South

In the meantime, Benjamin Church had gone to Plymouth on July 5 to get permission for the recently surrendered Saconnet warriors to join his company. The colony's council agreed. Church, Awashonks, and her people celebrated the new alliance with a grand feast along Buzzard's Bay, and by July 11 his force, with 140 Indians and 60 Englishmen, was storming through the area around Metacom's home territory, along the western edge of Plymouth. As his son later wrote, Church's "manner of Marching thro' the Woods was such, as if he were discovered, they appeared to be more than they were. For he always Marched at a wide distance one from another, partly for their safety: and this was an *Indian* custom [which he had adopted from his allies], to March thin and scatter."[2]

The use by Talcott, Church, and William Bradford of Native warriors and strategies became increasingly effective. Warriors surrendered throughout the summer, and some then agreed to fight with the English and help find their former comrades. On July 2, a large party surrendered in Cambridge, including the Christian Nipmuc James the Printer, who before the war had helped Eliot translate the Bible into Algonquian and during the war served as the scribe for the Narragansett and Nipmuc sachems. Increase Mather noted that James "did venture himself upon the mercy and truth of the English Declaration which he had seen and read, promising for the future to venture his life against the common Enemy." Indeed, Printer and his party were spared (unlike many others from Hassanamisset) even though many English considered him "a notorious Apostate" and "a false Villain." He went back to setting and working the press at Harvard College, and in a strange twist of fate he probably helped produce the first edition of Rowlandson's *Sovereignty and Goodness of God*.[3]

The English made it quite clear that Native leaders who sought clemency (for themselves and their warriors) had to spurn and even betray Metacom and others who seemed more dangerous. Some were quite ready to take that step. In early July, a group of four Nipmuc sachems who had been leaders in the prewar praying towns sent word to Boston authorities pledging to "make a Covenant of Peace with you . . . by *Jesus Christ*." Soon thereafter, Sagamore Sam, one of the four, informed Boston that Metacom and Quinnapin had left Wachusett because "they were much afraid, because of our offer to joyn with the *English*." He noted that when the two war leaders heard that the English were sending delegates, "*Philip* and *Quanapun* sent [word] to kill them; but I said, If any kill them, I'll kill them." About the same time, several other Nipmucs sent a note pledging that if the governor's council "had sent word to Kill Philip we should have done it."[4]

The first significant betrayal, however, was of the Nipmuc war leader Matoonas. On July 27, the Nipmuc sachem Sagamore John came to Boston with 180 of his people and, as a gift for the colony to win clemency, a bound and tied Matoonas and his son. Before the war Matoonas had served as constable in the praying town of Pakachoog and was believed to be "the beginner of the War in this Colony of Massachusetts" because he had been the first Nipmuc to join with Wampanoags in June 1675 and had led the assault on Mendon. The war sachem therefore represented to the Bay Colony all of the Indians' betrayal and treason.[5] After a short hearing, Massachusetts magistrates condemned the sachem and had John's men take Matoonas to the Commons, tie him to a tree, and shoot him.

As the summer of 1676 wore on, companies from Plymouth and Connecticut continued to mop up the remnants that had fled from Mount Wachusett to their homeland. The survivors still seemed to pose a danger to the colonists; on July 11, Bradford's forces (who had received warning) repelled an attack on Taunton. But the English had the clear advantage over the disheartened Indians, and during the next week the two companies killed hundreds of warriors who in small groups sought to hide in the area around Swansea, including on the seventeenth a band of about sixty near Pawtuxet.

At the end of July, a company of twenty-six Dedham and Medfield men joined by ten Christian Indians found Pumham and his Narragansett band, killed the sachem and many of his people, and took his son captive. On August 1, another company of colonists killed Metacom's lieutenant Nimrod while he was protecting his sachem's escape twelve miles northwest of Providence. Five days later, an Indian deserter entered Taunton and told the English about a nearby band; the men went out and captured about twenty-five Wampanoags. Some escaped, including Weetamoo, the "squaw sachem" of Pocasset, wife of the powerful Narragansett sachem Quinnapin and "mistress" of Mary Rowlandson. But shortly afterward her body was found in the Taunton River; apparently she had been shot and died or had drowned in the river. Plymouth leaders stuck her head on a pole in the center of Taunton. Local militia also occasionally went after the fugitives. But the most hunted Indian in the region was Metacom, the Wampanoag sachem who had come to symbolize all of the bloodshed and destruction of the war.

In early August, William Harris of Rhode Island described the sudden reversal of the war over the past four months and the terrible toll taken on the Indians who had fought the English. Since Canonchet had been killed in April, he noted, "two thousand Indians have been killed taken & come in . . . The Indians come in daily, and fight presently against the Indians they came from and betray one another into the hands of the English." The Connecticut militia was particularly active and tended to "kill all save boys & girls," and so the Indians were fleeing for their lives to Massachusetts and Rhode Island. Some actually went to those colonies to seek gunpowder in order to defend themselves against the Mohawks, "who kill & eat their enemies." But although the English forces and their allies were increasingly effective, more of the Indians had died "by sickness & hunger than by the sword." Harris estimated that about seven thousand Indians had died or been "transported" out of the region during the war.[6]

Metacom's Death

On July 24, Captain Benjamin Church received a special commission from Plymouth colony. He was given the charge to pursue Metacom, with the right to go anywhere in the colonies except Rhode Island, the power to appoint his officers, and the authority to offer amnesty to all who chose to abandon Metacom but the most notorious of the enemy leaders. Six days later, on a Sunday morning, he was attending church in Plymouth when Governor Winslow and a group of messengers rode into town with the alert that enemy warriors had been sighted near Bridgewater. Church immediately scrambled to assemble his company and by late afternoon was on the road to the village; that night they camped at Monponsett Pond.

The next morning, Bridgewater militia on their way to join Church's company surprised a group of warriors trying to cross the Taunton River on a felled tree. The colonists managed to shoot several and drove the others off, capturing guns and ammunition. One of those killed was Metacom's uncle, Unkompoin, and members of the militia saw Metacom at the crossing before most of the warriors escaped. The evidence from this skirmish indicated that Metacom and his people, along with some Narragansetts, were circling in a clockwise direction toward Mount Hope from Nipmuc territory via Bridgewater. Church's company arrived at Bridgewater that evening and made plans to move in pursuit the next morning with the town's militia.

Two days later, on the morning of August 1, the colonists again approached a large tree laid across the Taunton River. The boastful Church wrote in his journal, since lost but paraphrased decades later in a book published by his son, that he "spyd an Indian sitting upon the stump of it on the other side of the River; and he clap'd his Gun up, and had doubtless dispatch'd him, but that one of his own *Indians* called hastily to him, Not to fire, for he believed it was one of his own men; upon which the *Indian* upon the stump look'd about, and *Capt. Churches Indian* seeing his face perceived his mistake, for he knew him to be *Philip*."[7] Metacom immediately jumped down and fled, but Church's company managed to capture the sachem's wife Wootonekanuska and his nine-year-old son.

The captain left some men behind with the prisoners and ran after the escaping warriors. While the pursuers were unable to catch them, they found evidence that the Narragansetts led by Quinnapin were splitting off and heading for their tribal territory. This meant that Metacom was even more isolated with a smaller force. Some of Church's Native troops asked if they could continue after the Narragansetts because "*they wanted to be revenged on them for killing some of their Relations*."[8] He agreed and went back to his larger force with the prisoners. The chasers returned the following morning and reported that they had run them down, killed several, and taken thirteen prisoners.

Church's reunited company resumed stalking the fleeing Wampanoags. His advance guard found and captured a large number of women and children, who had been unable to keep up with the rapidly moving warriors, and then at sunset they found, surrounded, and captured a large group of men. In the morning he sent the prisoners back toward the larger, following force and dispatched two of his Native men forward to scout for the rest of Metacom's men. But at the same time, Metacom had sent two men back to see where the English lay. Those two saw Church's scouts and ran back to alert the sachem, who was forced to flee into the swamp without eating the breakfast he and his men had been preparing.

Church then split his force into two parts to run on each side of the swamp and meet at the other end; there they surprised and captured without a fight many men, women, and children as they emerged into the clearing, but Metacom was not among them. When the sachem discovered that those in the front had been captured, he and others "fled back upon his own Track."[9] Church had stationed a few soldiers at that end of the swamp, and when the shooting began he and three men ran into the swamp—and were nearly killed for their efforts. Metacom and the others escaped, but the colonists had captured 173 since the previous day. Some of the prisoners told Church that evening that Metacom was "*ready to dye . . . for you have now killed or taken all his Relations. That they believed he would now soon have his head, and that this bout had almost broke his heart.*"[10]

Church and his men returned to Bridgewater and Plymouth but were soon called out again to chase after Metacom and his remaining warriors, around Dartmouth and then over to Pocasset. At about the same time, an elderly, ill Wampanoag woman came into Sandwich to report that she had been with Metacom's infamous war sachem Totoson when he had died, supposedly from a broken heart after finding his son sick and near death—but then she died before showing the burial place. A major break came on August 11, when a Wampanoag contacted the English at the fort across from Mount Hope. He told them that Metacom had killed his brother "*for giving some advice that displeased him,*" that he had fled to escape the same fate, and that the sachem was at that moment camped on Mount Hope Neck. The colonists sent two men to fetch Church, who went with his company to meet the man.

The bitter warrior agreed to direct Church to the sachem on the southwest side of Mount Hope. The small party got into small boats to cross over to the peninsula, and the Wampanoag led them to the edge of the swamp where Metacom was camped. At dawn on the twelfth, Church laid out a trap. A small group at one end would move quietly toward the camp, and at a prearranged moment they would rise up and fire with the goal of alarming the Indians and getting them to flee. He stationed his other men at regular intervals along most of the rest of the swamp, in each case putting a colonist and an Indian together, "knowing it was *Philips* custom to be foremost in the flight." But as Captain Roger Goulding crawled up to the camp, he suddenly saw a Wampanoag "going forth to ease himself"—to urinate—and, thinking he had been seen, fired his musket.[11] Goulding's men then fired as well, and Metacom and the others grabbed their weapons and sprinted for safety. But the sachem unknowingly headed right for an ambush. The Englishman's weapon misfired, but the Indian, Alderman, managed to shoot twice, killing Metacom.

Alderman went to tell Church, who asked him to keep the news to himself while the others searched the rest of the swamp for survivors. But only four other Wampanoags had been victims of the ambush; the great war sachem Annawan had escaped, as had most of the warriors camped there. Church then summoned "his old *Indian* executioner," who said of Metacom that "*He*

had been *a very great man, and had made many a man afraid of him, but so big as
he was, he would now chop his arse for him.*"[12] The man beheaded and quartered
Metacom; Church hung each quarter in a different tree and gave a hand to
Alderman, who earned money by showing it around the colonies, supposedly
preserved in a bucket of rum. When Plymouth authorities heard the news,
they called for a day of thanksgiving on August 17; soon after the Reverend
John Cotton finished his sermon, Church arrived with the sachem's head,
which was paraded through the town and then put on a tall post for all of the
colonists to view and revile.

Defeat and Revenge

After the death of Metacom on August 12, the final act of the war in the
southeast was Church's capture of Annawan, war chief and a Wampanoag
leader since Massasoit's time. In late August, the Plymouth captain learned
from captured Wampanoags that Annawan's band was camped in a nearby
swamp. On the evening of August 28, Church's company entered the swamp
at Rehoboth, Massachusetts, and he decided to approach the camp from behind by descending the face of a cliff and then having an elderly Indian man
and the man's daughter—who had told him of Annawan's location—go in
front so (Church wrote later) the war leader would not notice the plot. When
Church darted out and seized the stacked weapons, Annawan gave up without a fight and, seemingly impressed with Church's courage and daring, had
his women prepare dinner for them to eat together.

At the end of the night, Annawan went and retrieved the wampum belts
that Metacom had worn around his body and head and handed them to
Church, telling him "in plain *English*" that "you have killed *Philip* and conquered his Country, for I believe that I & my company are the last that War
against the English, so suppose the War is ended by your means, and therefore
these things belong to you."[13] In the morning, Church marched Annawan and
his band to Taunton. The colonists beheaded the Wampanoag war chief a
few days later. The following spring, Governor Winslow sent the belts and
Metacom's other possessions to the king of England; the items disappeared
and have never been found.

As the enemy scattered, fled attacks, and sought clemency or even to join
the colonial forces, the increasingly confident colonies passed laws authorizing capital punishment for surrendering Indians. In English eyes, Natives

who had fought against them were traitors and criminals. War leaders like Annawan were quickly put to death. Those who had been officers of praying towns and were thought to have joined the enemy were viewed as particularly monstrous for having betrayed God as well as the English. Some like James the Printer were spared. But others were not so fortunate. For example, Captain Tom (Wuttasacomponom), before the war a judge at Hassanamisset, was executed despite a petition from James Quannapohit and others who fought for the English telling the Massachusetts Council that Tom (like Printer and others from that village) had been taken and kept "against their wills" by the enemy.[14]

Throughout the summer and fall, the huge execution oak on Boston Common was put to heavy use. On June 22, Captain Tom and another Christian Indian were hung from it, "penitent, praying to God, not like the manner of the heathen."[15] In late July, Matoonas was tied to it and shot by Sagamore John's warriors. In August and September, about forty-five prisoners were hung or shot there. Several other Christian Indians were, like Captain Tom, hung from the tree, most prominently Old Jethro, who had been the preacher at Nashaway before the war.

The victors even felt free to ignore pardons. The Narragansett sachem Potuck had, in early July, gone to Rhode Island seeking to surrender and was granted safe conduct and clemency to go to Newport to negotiate terms. Instead, he was taken to Boston, tried and found guilty of war crimes, and on August 4 shot on the Commons. Monoco surrendered to Richard Waldron after the New Hampshire trader and officer promised the fugitive pardon, and the two Nipmuc sachems Muttawmp and Sagamore John (Shoshonin) who brought him to Waldron—and who had led successful attacks and devastated colonial forces at New Braintree, Brookfield, Bloody Brook, and Sudbury—were similarly promised amnesty. But all three were sent to Boston, where Massachusetts authorities executed them in late September 1676. That same month, Metacom's brother-in-law Tispaquin surrendered to Benjamin Church after getting assurances that he and his men would be given amnesty and enlisted to fight alongside the English in Maine—but the "Black Sachem" was immediately shot by Plymouth authorities. Similarly, on August 25, the Narragansett sachem Quinnapin (Weetamoo's husband and Mary Rowlandson's master) was shot at Newport even though he had been given quarter when he surrendered.

The English were not the only ones taking revenge on the defeated. The

Mohegans had for decades sparred with the Narragansetts, and that summer they found the opportunity to pursue that quarrel with the blessings of the colonists. On July 2, after they had helped Connecticut troops destroy a village and kill 171—mostly women and children—the tribe's warriors asked to torture and kill "a young sprightly Fellow." The colonists agreed, in part to please "their *Indian* Friends" and in part so they might witness "the Salvage, barbarous Cruelty of these Heathen." In keeping with Eastern Woodlands norms, when the prisoner realized his fate, he did not beg for mercy but boasted of the nineteen Englishmen he had "dispatched" and the Mohegan he had killed that morning.

The Mohegans encircled the captive and began taking him apart. They "cut one of his Fingers round in the joint, at the Trunk of his Hand, with a sharp Knife, and then brake it oft," repeating this until one hand was completely destroyed, with "the Blood sometimes spitting out in Streams a Yard from his Hand." The English watchers were fascinated and repelled, particularly that the man being tortured never showed pain or distress. "For being asked by some of his Tormentors, how he liked the War? . . . this insensible and hardhearted Monster answered, He liked it very well, and found it as sweet, as English Men did their Sugar. In this Frame he continued, till his Executioners had dealt with the Toes of his Feet, as they had done with the Fingers of his Hands; all the while making him Dance round the Circle, and Sing, till he had wearied both himself and them. At last *they* broke the Bones of his Legs, after which he was forced to sit down, which 'tis said he silently did, till they had knocked out his Brains."[16]

Many of those not executed were sold into slavery by the colonists. Enslavement began during the war, and John Eliot argued that this was bad policy because it would keep many Indians from surrendering and thereby extend the war. But most ministers and magistrates disagreed, noting that the Bible justified making slaves of war captives, and the Natives would be useful in obtaining African slaves. Many Indian children were placed into servitude with colonists (including Daniel Gookin) until age twenty, including the thirty-four who surrendered with Sagamore Sam. Captives of all ages and both sexes were purchased by prominent Massachusetts officials (such as Samuel Shrimpton and Samuel Appleton) and officers (such as Daniel Henchman and Samuel Moseley). In September 1676, the governors of Massachusetts and Plymouth justified enslavement and the shipping of at least 180 men, women, and children to Jamaica aboard the *Seaflower* by pointing to

Metacom's betrayal of his treaties with the colonists and his resulting treason against the king's sovereignty.

There was particular debate among New England ministers over what to do with Metacom's young son, who was being held along with his mother in a Plymouth prison. Samuel Arnold and John Cotton ruled that Deuteronomy 24:16 forbade holding the child responsible for his father's crimes, while Increase Mather thought that other biblical incidents provided moral precedents for executing the boy. Finally, in March 1677, Cotton noted in a letter to Mather that "Philips boy goes now to be sold"—where and to whom, there is no record. The majority of captives, possibly more than a thousand, were transported to the West Indies, Bermuda, and even North Africa; most quickly died on the terrible sugar plantations, although some passed their memories to their descendants.

Some of the warriors and their families who had been at Wachusett or Squakeag headed west or north instead of east, seeking refuge in new places instead of hoping for mercy in the southeast. In May 1676, Governor Andros of New York had issued a proclamation declaring that New England Indians would be welcome to settle at Schaghticoke, a Mahican village where the Hoosic and Tomhannock rivers meet that already had a history of hosting refugees from various tribes. For Andros this was a way to gain at the expense of Massachusetts and Connecticut, and for the Mohawks who dominated the area this offered an influx of new people and connections, which (in the context of Eastern Woodlands diplomacy and culture) meant more power. A few months after Metacom's death, the governor held a welcoming conference at Schaghticoke with Dutch, English, Mohawks, Mahicans, and New England Indian refugees and planted a ceremonial tree of peace. Not all of the Indians escaping the conflagration went there; some headed north and found refuge among the Wabanakis.

War Renewed in the North

Even as the colonists began to relax with the news of Native warriors surrendering in ever-larger numbers to Anglo-Indian patrols, the war in the north, which had seemed to end with the winter, erupted again. On a late afternoon on Tuesday, August 11, a Wabanaki band led by Simon (who became known as "the Yankee Killer" and may have been a Christian) gained entrance to Anthony Bracket's house in Falmouth on Casco Bay by brandishing a pass issued by the English commander. In the morning, at almost the very moment of Metacom's death, Simon "pulled off his Vizour of a Friend": his men seized "all the Guns they could see," took the unfortunate Brackets captive, and attacked the neighboring houses.[17] By the time they were done, they had killed or taken captive thirty-four settlers. For another year the war would rage in the north as Wabanakis hit villages and outposts throughout coastal Maine, gaining victories and many captives with their effective tactics, and the colonists were again forced to abandon their homes and flee south.

The stories and anger that the Nipmuc and other refugees carried north seem to have spurred the Wabanakis to renew their war against the English. But the Natives in the region had their own reasons. During the spring, a colonist had kidnapped and sold into slavery several Indians, claiming license to punish those who had committed "Murder or Spoil" in the fall—but he took them from the Cape Sable area, not where the "hostiles" lived. The Wabanaki sachems made "many Complaints" about "the *hard dealing* of the English" traders along the Kennebec River. And settlers in the region continued to commit trespass on Native lands, poach their fish and game, and earn their reputation for lawlessness. John Earthy, who supervised trade and settlement around Pemaquid, north of Casco Bay, managed in the spring to keep the peace despite "the *Violence* used by some refractory *English*." William Hubbard scornfully observed that the colonists wanted "to shake off all Yoke of Government, both sacred and civil," and certainly they resisted efforts by Massachusetts to exert its authority in the region. In an August conference at Pemaquid, the Wabanaki sachems were "offended" when Massachusetts representatives refused to return their guns and confirmed the ban on selling them gunpowder and shot.[18]

On August 14, two days after Simon's band had successfully infiltrated and attacked Falmouth, a small group of Indians gained entrance to the home of Richard Hammond along the east side of the Kennebec River, in modern Woolrich. Hammond was "an ancient Inhabitant and Trader" with a reputation for cheating the Kennebecs, and he was immediately killed; the fifteen members of his family were also killed or captured and died later.[19] The successful warriors divided into two groups, one of which traveled to Arrowsic Island, where the next day they seized and destroyed a trading post—a small village, really, with six outbuildings, a huge warehouse, a mansion, and a mill—owned by two Boston merchants, Captain Thomas Clarke and Captain Thomas Lake. Lake, along with Sylvanus Davis and two others, escaped out the back, but Lake was later killed and Davis badly wounded by pursuers. The English at Pemaquid, fearing attack, burned and abandoned the garrison.

Several weeks later, Wabanaki warriors took a supposedly secure garrison on Jewells Island in Casco Bay. By the end of the month, the English had almost completely abandoned the region northeast of Scarborough; many headed for Salem, where they had relatives or could easily find refuge. The settlers were reluctant to stand their ground against these attacks, at least in part because Boston had relatively little authority in Maine, and the United Colonies was ineffective in this part of the war because other colonies and well-connected English speculators continued to challenge the Puritan colony's claim to the region.

As the northeastern front erupted, Boston dispatched men to Richard Waldron, the regional military commander, including Wampanoag and Massachusett units commanded by Benjamin Church. Waldron was a leading Indian trader in New Hampshire and operated out of his garrisoned home in Quechecho, on the Piscataqua River. While he knew Native people and their language, his reputation for cheating was such that it was still strong in the mid-nineteenth century. Set loose by the colony, he pursued a scorched-earth strategy that gave no quarter and rarely distinguished between friend and foe.

One incident became particularly notorious. By early September, nearly four hundred Natives were camping near Quechecho, primarily in order to avoid the fighting to the north. Waldron received orders to search for and capture any and all southern New England Indians who might have found refuge among the Wabanakis. To accomplish this, on September 7, 1676, Waldron invited the Natives to a peace conference at his home, told them that the English planned to take many warriors into their army, and gave them rum to celebrate. When they became drunk, his armed men surrounded them, and Waldron and his officers separated those that they thought were guilty and sent them to Boston, where some were executed and the rest enslaved— including some Christian Indians with relatives fighting for the English. This betrayal caused deep, lasting anger; some of the Natives who attacked Deerfield in 1704 said that that was their revenge.

The Wabanakis continued their attacks, and English efforts to stop them were notably unsuccessful. On October 12, the Kennebec sachem Mugg Hegone appeared outside the Black Point garrison with about seventy-five warriors painted and armed for war. The commander, Captain Joshua Scottow,

was in Boston dealing with recent legal and political problems, so Henry Jocelyn, owner of the garrison, went out to talk with Hegone, who "had from
a *Child* been well acquainted with the English, and had lived some Years in
English Families."[20] After a long negotiation, Jocelyn returned with Hegone's
offer of a peaceful surrender—but found that all of the men had quietly left
out the back and fled south while he was talking with the sachem. The Wabanakis had driven nearly all of the English from their territory.

Hegone and his Penobscot ally Madockawando hoped to use the victory to
obtain a favorable peace agreement with Massachusetts. In November, Mugg
boarded a ship sent by Boston to bring him down to the capital to negotiate
"a *firm Peace* . . . in the Name of *Madockawando*, the Chief of all the Indians
in the Eastern Parts about Penobscot."[21] As usual, the English hoped that a
particular sachem could command like a king, an assumption that was usually wrong, particularly for decentralized societies like the Wabanakis. The
colonial authorities insisted on very strict terms, including reparations for
damages done to settler property and the return of all English captives, many
of whom were held by groups over which the two sachems had no authority.
While both men released their captives, Mugg was unsuccessful at quickly
persuading another Native group (who he feared would kill or capture him)
to send back the English they had taken.

Wabanaki trust dipped lower in late February 1677 when, at a conference
with Penobscot sachems to discuss peace, Waldron again used deception to
disarm and seize the Indian leaders. These events sent many Indian refugees
deep into the interior, settling at Schaghticoke and St. Francis (Odanak) in
Quebec, and ensured that the war would continue as a series of small-scale
raids against English settlements. In April, Simon raided York and Wells, killing ten. Beginning on May 14, Mugg Hegone and his warriors once again besieged the garrison at Black Point, which had been reoccupied by the English;
this time the attackers would find the defenses too difficult, and Hegone was
killed on May 16. The warriors withdrew and doubled back to hit York and
Wells again, killing seven. That summer, the Wabanakis successfully stole
twenty English fishing boats from Salem that were anchored in Maine waters;
the raiders stripped and abandoned the ships. English raids against Indian
villages, on the other hand, found only empty villages, as their inhabitants
retreated into the woods.

A settlement of the conflict required, as with the war in the south, the involvement of the Iroquois and the New York governor. In June 1677, Andros

led an expedition that took control of Pemaquid Fort and the surrounding Sagadahoc Province, supposedly because he feared that it might be seized by the French, but probably in large part to intimidate the Puritan colony. Massachusetts was too weak to object. That spring, Massachusetts delegates obtained a promise by the Mohawks to enter the war. Perhaps as a result of the Mohawk threat and New York's soothing presence, in July the Kennebecs sent back twenty English captives and asked Bay Colony authorities for a truce and treaty—and told Boston that, had it not been for Waldron's deceptions, they would have returned the prisoners long ago. They were met with a bland promise that the abuses of the past would be solved by more orderly English settlement in the future. The Wabanakis turned instead to Sagadahoc, whose commanders brokered a truce in August 1677, formalized in the Casco Treaty of April 1678.

As an uneasy peace settled in the region, many Wabanakis began returning to the region in a pattern that would become common as subsequent wars rocked the region. Fifteen years later, some of the English refugees from Maine would be accusers or defendants in the Salem witchcraft trials. But this was the end of only the first wave of warfare in northern New England. At the end of the century, Native anger would again explode. King William's War in 1689 would begin with the successful deception by Wabanaki women opening the door to Waldron's garrison and his death by torture at the hands of the attackers—payment for his deceptions a decade before. The warfare would not end completely until the conclusion of the French and Indian War in 1760.

Suffering for Survivors

King Philip's War was the bloodiest war in American history in terms of its proportionate effect on a region. Of the approximately eighty thousand people living in the region in May 1675, nearly nine thousand (over 10%) were killed; one-third of the casualties were English and two-thirds were Native. The political and cultural effects on the people in the region were perhaps even more significant and longer lasting, creating scarred memories that still rankled 150 years later.

The consequences of the war for Natives in southern New England were most severe. Their numbers decreased by about half, from 25 percent to only about 10 percent of the human population in the region. About three thousand died from combat, disease, or hunger; perhaps two thousand refugees left the region, heading west for New York or north toward New France; and about one thousand were sold into slavery and certain death in the West Indies. In 1698, six years after Plymouth was annexed to Massachusetts, that colony counted 4,168 Indians. Perhaps the most significant result of the war was the end of Indian sovereignty east of the Connecticut River.

In May 1676, as the war in the south ground to a close, the Christian Indians were released from internment on Deer Island; most went to live near Waban's original village of Nonantum. On August 7, three women and three children went to pick berries on a hill near Concord. They were accompanied by a guard, John Stoolemester, a Christian Indian who had recently been mustered out of the army. As the berry pickers worked their way across the hill, Stoolemester was confronted by a group of English horsemen. They threatened to kill him but were persuaded that he had indeed served with the colonial military and let him go. The English found the berry pickers Stoolemester had described, talked with them, and went on. But four of the men returned and murdered all six, shooting some and brutally beating others with hatchets. Although in this instance the murderers were convicted and sentenced to death, the Natives who remained in the region continued to suffer from prejudice, poverty, and a marginal legal status, still they did survive and maintained various communities in the region on reserves set aside by provincial acts.

In Massachusetts, Christian Indians were kept from their villages for many years because of the bitter opposition of white neighbors and the continued threat of raids by Mohawks, although by the 1690s they resettled four praying towns, with Natick again the largest. Those in Plymouth experienced fewer disruptions, but as colonial towns expanded they were forced to move to larger villages with land reserved under provincial law, particularly Mashpee on Cape Cod and Gay Head on Martha's Vineyard. In Connecticut, Uncas and his Mohegans retained a fair degree of power and substantial lands as a result of their connections with important Connecticut leaders and service in the war. But after Uncas's death in 1683, the colony began granting Mohegan lands to towns and speculators, and the tribe's lawsuit against those actions traveled around the English courts until it finally died in 1773. In Rhode Island, Ninigret's territory became an oasis of Indian autonomy and his Narragansett tribe became the largest in the region. But the sachem's successors sold nearly all of their lands to the colony.

All of these tribes remained semiautonomous, helped by provincial laws that made it illegal for Indians to sell their lands without the permission of the assembly. But they were also closely connected to provincial politics and law. For example, Connecticut chose or "blessed" Mohegan and Pequot sachems, Rhode Island authorities "helped" the Narragansett sachems with their affairs, and Massachusetts appointed guardians to oversee Indian groups and their resources. And when conflicts erupted between a particular tribe and local residents, or with a guardian or justice of the peace, the Indians sought assistance within the legal and political systems. But despite this potential support, Native communities continued to be injured by prejudice, indebtedness, and a marginal social status and battered by epidemics and alcoholism. The survivors adapted by teetering along the line between isolation from and immersion in colonial society and culture, seeking to satisfy their needs in the new environment while maintaining critical boundaries against white settlers. Growing numbers of Indian men worked as mariners and whalers, many young women worked as domestics in colonial households, and children served long periods of indentures.

New England Indian men did manage to maintain their warrior traditions by serving in the colonial militia on the Maine frontier. For example, in 1704, at the outbreak of Queen Anne's War, about two-thirds of the 150 adult Mohegan men were serving in the Connecticut military. Provincial officials saw the Indians as invaluable additions to frontier defense, and their officers, including Benjamin Church and his sons, negotiated with tribes in ways that recognized Native leadership, autonomy, and culture. Often recruiters would need to provide a feast and needed supplies and followed traditional diplomatic protocols, all at provincial expense. The men who enlisted not only earned significant wages and bounties for themselves and their families, income that was otherwise unavailable to Indians, but also could gain prestige in the traditional warrior mode. They also enlisted in groups, formed separate Indian companies ranging in size from 20 to 150 men, and were often allowed to choose their own officers.

Christianity became an even more significant aspect of Indian life, and the church became their religious and social center. In Massachusetts, Native ministers rose in prominence and authority: they served as political as well as spiritual leaders and knit together scattered Native communities into networks. Natives in Connecticut and Rhode Island continued to resist the occasional missionary, but in the 1740s, the Mohegans, Niantics, Pequots, and

Narragansetts enthusiastically embraced the radical evangelical elements of the Great Awakening, formed their own churches, and developed a host of talented and famous Native ministers. After the American Revolution, they would lead many of their people west in the Brothertown movement.

Hardships for Victors

The colonists were badly mauled by the conflict, particularly in Massachusetts, where most of the raids occurred and the war continued in the north until 1677. Thousands lost their relatives and became refugees. Of ninety towns in New England, fifty-two (58%) were attacked, twenty-five pillaged (over 25%), and seventeen razed. These figures do not include the many outposts (like the Clark garrison near Plymouth) that were burned or abandoned. Nearly all of the towns in Massachusetts twenty miles or more west of Boston were abandoned. In the Connecticut River valley, New Hampshire, and Maine, the threat of raids continued, flaring into open war during King William's War (1689–99), Queen Anne's War (1704–13), Dummer's War (1722–24), King George's War (1744–48), and the Seven Years or French and Indian War (1754–60).

In the wake of the war, the New England colonists resumed their rapid population growth, increasing tenfold over the next century, mostly from natural increase rather than immigration. Their economic and geographic expansion did not, however, increase in a similar fashion. Massachusetts and particularly Boston did expand its fishing fleet and commercial connections with the British empire, creating a shipbuilding industry and dominating the carrying trade in the North American colonies. Yet per capita income in the region did not return to 1675 levels until after the development of industry in the early 1800s, and Massachusetts colonists did not resettle villages abandoned during the war because of the continued threat of western Wabanaki raids. In addition, the Christian Nipmucs who went to Natick after the war had come from villages in that area, and Massachusetts authorities felt it necessary to settle their claims in the region, particularly since Connecticut and Plymouth pressed competing claims and the Crown's growing challenge to the Massachusetts Charter endangered unilateral grants made by the General Court. In the 1680s, the colony negotiated a series of deeds with Nipmucs that transferred nearly all of the territory in the middle of the region to Massachusetts. But few colonists dared settle in that area until after the 1713 Treaty of Utrecht, which seemed to halt French encouragement of Native raids against the English.

While the coalition led by Massachusetts won the war in the south, that colony in the wake of its victory also lost much of its sovereignty. Even before Massachusetts asked the Crown for monetary assistance in April, King Charles II had decided to send Edward Randolph—who had headed the 1664 commission so critical of the Puritan colony—to look into the litany of Quaker and other complaints and to bring the colony to heel. Randolph arrived in Boston in June, opening a political struggle there and in London over who would control the province. As befitted the Puritan colony's history, this conflict had a religious element: Randolph's chaplain immediately performed a wedding using the Church of England's *Book of Common Prayer*, which the colony had banned. The colony's council tried to avoid dealing directly with the envoy, so in July Randolph urged the secretary of state in London to send warships to blockade Boston and force them into submission to the Crown. But the colony was lucky: Charles had at that moment more significant issues to deal with than a small colony in an isolated corner of the empire.

In 1682, the Crown formally challenged the Massachusetts charter in *quo warranto* proceedings, which encouraged dissidents in and outside the colony. Four years later, the colony lost its charter and was folded into the Dominion of New England, along with all of the northeastern colonies, including Plymouth, Connecticut, New York, and New Jersey. The king barred assemblies from meeting and named Sir Edmund Andros as governor-general of the Dominion. When Andros arrived in Boston to set up his government, he challenged many of the past actions by New England colonies, including the granting of town charters. This threat caused many town leaders, particularly in Massachusetts, to seek deeds to their lands from Indian survivors in the region, confirming grants supposedly made decades earlier. In late 1688, rumors of the Glorious Revolution in England led Boston Puritans to overthrow Andros, and a few years later Massachusetts would regain some autonomy and (ironically) annex Plymouth with a new charter from the new king. But the Bay Colony would never reclaim the sovereignty held before the war.

⚕ Epilogue

NEW ENGLANDERS BEGAN arguing over the meaning and memory of King Philip's War even before it ended. In December 1675, Nathaniel Saltonstall published in London *The Present State of New-England with Respect to the Indian War*, which presented a sparse list of the terrible events. John Easton circulated a manuscript of his "Relacion of the Indyan War" with its sympathetic depiction of Metacom. Three months before Metacom's death, Increase Mather, the Bay Colony's intellectual and political leader, began writing a history to depict the war as punishment for the colonists' sins, including men wearing long hair, excessive greed, and not doing enough to convert the Indians. Mather's *A Brief History of the Warr with the Indians in New-England* would be published in fall 1676 in Boston and London.

The following spring, William Hubbard, minister at Ipswich and Mather's competitor, published a very different *Narrative of the Troubles with the Indians in New-England*, which depicted essentialist differences between the Natives and the English in moral and racial terms. The other significant contemporary depiction of the war, Mary Rowlandson's *Sovereignty and Goodness of God* (1682), presented a view of the Christian and the enemy Indians closer to

Hubbard's than Mather's; her work served as the prototype for thousands of eighteenth- and nineteenth-century American captivity narratives.

Despite their disagreements about the causes and nature of the war, all of these writers shared one thing: they were English. Neither the Indians who fought the English nor those who fought for the colonists left any writings about the war explaining their reasons or experiences. Rowlandson's book and other narratives of the war would be republished in the 1770s, as New Englanders looked to their past to better understand the current threat from the British "savages" threatening their lands and liberties.

A half century later, a clear shift occurred in how Americans viewed Metacom, King Philip's War, and New England's colonial past. This change was driven by the blossoming of literature that often included the romantic image of the Noble Indian and became an archetype in 1826 with James Fenimore Cooper's *Last of the Mohicans*. It began with Washington Irving's "Philip of Pokanoket," published in the *Analectic Magazine* in 1814, which recast Metacom as "a true born prince, gallantly fighting . . . to deliver his native land from the oppression of usurping strangers." A few years later, *Yamoyden* by James Eastburn and Robert Charles Sands cast the Natives as suffering "foul oppressions" from the Puritans who reeked of "soulless bigotry" and "avarice."[1] That poem inspired Lydia Maria Francis of Boston to write *Hobomok*, which in 1824 became a best seller, replete with noble and virtuous Indians and severe, dour Puritans.

Northern critics of the emerging U.S. Indian Removal policy found this romantic, revisionist history of King Philip's War particularly appealing. Although Sarah Savage's *Life of Philip* (1827), a sentimentalist novel written for children and adults, called the "revered" Puritans' intentions "just, and even kind," it condemned contemporary U.S. Indian policies and noted that "there seems now no possible excuse for advancing upon Indian lands. We are great, powerful, and rich."[2] Lydia Marie Francis's next book, *First Settlers of New England* (1829), savaged the Puritans as intolerant hypocrites and, in the introduction, told readers that she wished to show how such evil treatment of Indians continued in federal policy and, if not reversed, would inevitably doom America "to the calamitous reverses which have fallen on other nations."[3]

This revisionist history of abused New England Indians became a new standard. In 1827, Samuel Goodrich, one of the earliest publishers of school books, published *Tales of Peter Palfrey about America*, which told America's history through this fictional character. Palfrey grew up in Boston in the mid-eighteenth century, was friends with an Indian chief, and witnessed a massacre by whites of a peaceful Indian village. Two years later, the already-famous American actor Edwin Forrest began performing the title role in the play he had commissioned, *Metamora; or, The Last of the Wampanoags*. The heroic but doomed Metamora became a national passion as Forrest took the play to every city and state over the following two decades. Audiences wept as Philip's wife and child were captured by hostile Puritans, and at the conclusion of the play they "rose in wild and reportedly 'rapturous' applause" when the mortally wounded sachem cried "curses on you, white men! The last of the Wampanoags' curse be on you!"[4] It was so popular that many delegations of western Indian tribes visiting American cities in the 1830s and 1840s were taken to see the play.

But this sympathy for Metacom and Indian resistance did not mean that New Englanders were ready to restore land or give more sovereignty to Indian descendants in the region, many still living in their ancestral communities. Instead, Americans generally viewed the defeat of the Wampanoags and their allies as inevitable and necessary and either ignored the survivors and their descendants or depicted them as a vanishing people. In August 1876, in a special celebration of the two hundredth anniversary of Metacom's death, Rhode Island's governor described the sachem's resistance as just but doomed to fail, and he added (as so many noted in other anniversary celebrations) that the few remaining Indians in the region would soon be extinct.[5]

Indian Memories of the War

In the audience listening to the governor were Melinda and Charlotte Mitchell, daughters of Zervia Gould Mitchell, who had become celebrities as lineal descendants of Massasoit (and therefore Metacom) and were using this fame to press their claim to Wampanoag lands in Bristol County, Massachusetts, and to sell baskets and other crafts to those attending the festival. Their presence pointed to the question of how Indian families and communities in southern New England remembered King Philip's War. But as subaltern, marginalized people, Indians kept those memories among themselves. There were some occasional glimpses. In the eighteenth century, Metacom's skull disappeared; one recorded story is that Wampanoags stole it and buried it secretly, and that it still occasionally speaks to those who know where to find it. Furthermore, in January 1836, the Pequot minister William Apess gave a speech that condemned the fraud and intolerance of the Puritans and celebrated the "immortal Philip . . . held in memory by the degraded but yet grateful descendants of Wampanoags," as an equal to "the immortal George Washington."[6] Boston elites at the city's Odeon Theater warmly applauded this condemnation of their ancestors and tribute to the man who sought to kill them.

After the Civil War, Connecticut, Massachusetts, and Rhode Island eliminated the laws that offered some protection for Indian lands and handicaps for individual Natives. State leaders were inspired by the ideal of equality and the racist notion that, owing to generations of acculturation and intermarriage with blacks and whites, no "real" Indians remained in the region. Shortly after, many towns in the region began organizing elaborate pageants that celebrated their founding and often invited delegations from Indian groups in the region to participate. The organizers and observers saw the Indians as a people who were nearly extinct, vanishing or displaced by a more civilized race. But those Indians used their participation to organize their people and wear traditional costume to confirm their tribal identity. After 1925, their children and grandchildren would seek to revive their tribes through pow-wows (dance and social events) and community institutions.

In the context of this tribal renaissance, the sites and stories of King Philip's War became places and opportunities for Native peoples in southern New England to reclaim history and power. Narragansetts tell that, in 1675, they "allied themselves with King Philip and the Wampanoag Sachem, to support the Wampanoag Tribe's efforts to reclaim land in Massachusetts." After "the Great Swamp Massacre," many who survived "retreated deep into the forest and swamp lands" that "now makes up today's Reservation," and "any who refused to be subjected to the authority of the United Colonies left the area or were hunted down and killed. Some were sold into slavery in the Caribbean, others migrated to upstate New York and many went to Brotherton, Wisconsin."[7] Mashpees tell that "the increase of voracious, marauding colonists" generated the conflict that drove Metacom to organize "an alliance of New England Tribes against . . . seizure of Indian Territory and attacks on personal liberties."[8] And Nipmucs emphasize their imprisonment on Deer Island, noting that "hundreds died and few ever returned to their native lands," and that they "return annually to Deer Island to mourn their ancestors."[9]

Since the mid-1970s, nearly all of the New England Indian groups that remained in the nineteenth century have sought formal recognition as tribes by the federal government. A few, such as the Mashantucket Pequots, achieved it through special acts of Congress; some, such as the Narragansetts and Mashpee Wampanoags, were rewarded that status through the BIA's Federal Acknowledgement process; and others, such as the Hassanamisco (Hassanamisset) Nipmucs, were denied or are still seeking recognition. Although some groups had state charters or other official status, federal acknowledgement offers emotional and institutional validation, substantial financial assistance, and the right to open and operate casinos. It also means that the tribe can recover some of what it lost in King Philip's War: a higher level of sovereignty, the power to protect existing resources, and the ability to regain sacred and significant lands.

The Significance of King Philip's War

The war made the Puritan colonies far more vulnerable to rule by the Crown within the emerging imperial structure, leading directly to King James II revoking the Massachusetts charter and his creation of the Dominion of New England in 1685. In the wake of the Glorious Revolution, Massachusetts would get a new charter and Plymouth, but never the sovereignty it held before the war. Connecticut and Rhode Island recovered more autonomy than the Bay Colony, but all of the colonies continued to be more closely monitored by England. One historian called King Philip's War and its aftermath (along with Bacon's Rebellion in Virginia) "the end of American independence," and more broadly scholars consider the conflict the end of the Puritan ideal that their "errand into the wilderness" was to establish God's commonwealth as an example for the rest of Christendom.[10] The cultural significance of this shift can be glimpsed in the emergence of the New England jeremiad, a sermon in which ministers blamed troubles from earthquakes to epidemics to disobedient children on their backsliding parishioners.

King Philip's War fundamentally reshaped the human, cultural, and political landscape of southern New England. The conflict destroyed most of the Natives and left the survivors clearly subordinate to colonial authority. But the colonists were also badly mauled by the war, particularly in Massachusetts, where most of the raids occurred and where the war continued in the north for a year after Metacom's death. Not surprisingly, the war became a fundamental turning point in relations between Anglo-Americans and

Natives. As towns burned, Puritan writers began to portray the Natives as subhuman demons in popular histories that blazed the short path of hatred to the occasional nineteenth-century efforts to exterminate Indians. Mary Rowlandson's story continued to sell well into the eighteenth century and set the pattern for the subsequent avalanche of captivity narratives, which became one of the most popular literary genres in America and went on to shape how Hollywood movies depicted Indians. Many of the Americans who traveled to Oregon or California in the mid-nineteenth century were raised with these histories, which (unfortunately) shaped what they expected and how they reacted when they actually met Natives along the trail. Finally, this war became, ironically, the first Indian defense of land and sovereignty to be celebrated instead of condemned by the descendants of the victors.

The war's long development and extensive documentation made it the prototype for what became a long history of conflicts between Natives and Anglo-Americans. While there were previous explosions over resources, such as the Pequot War and the earlier (1622) Powhatan uprising in Virginia, this was the first war driven by the irresolvable clash between Native and colonial claims to sovereignty, the colonists' insistence that disagreements be judged by their legal system and standards, and the unwillingness of the colonists to accommodate Native cultures, economies, and land use. All of these elements can be found in most if not all of the subsequent major wars between Natives and settlers during the next two centuries of American expansion. Most also ended the same way, with the settlers initially suffering disastrous defeats but then wearing down and destroying their enemies, and then either enslaving or subjugating the survivors on reservations. And as happened in King Philip's War, Natives who remained neutral or even cast their lot with the settlers played an important role in the ultimate course of the conflict. But despite this critical assistance, the victors by and large treated all Indians poorly in the end.

ACKNOWLEDGMENTS

William Keegan, history mapmaker supreme, has been a close partner in this work. Bill did more than "simply" create the very new and informative maps that are so important for the book; he asked questions and brought new information to my attention that helped me rethink places, movements, communities, and other aspects of southern New England in the last half of the eighteenth century. I can't thank you enough, Bill.

Less immediate but still significant assistance came from Alden Vaughan and Randy Boehm, who asked me to edit the *New England Treaties, Southeast* volume (no. 19) in the series *Early American Indian Documents: Treaties and Laws, 1607–1789* (University Press of America, 2003). Assembling, editing, and annotating the documents for that volume served as a springboard for my subsequent work on King Philip's War. Several years later, Paul Rosier asked me to write a book on the war in a series for secondary school students; *King Philip's War: The Conflict over New England* was published by Chelsea House in 2007. Christian Green at Chelsea House then gave me approval to write this substantially different work for this Johns Hopkins University Press series.

NOTES

Prologue

1. Until the mid-eighteenth century, England and its colonies used the Julian calendar, which had the year begin on March 25, so at the time the date would have been written March 22, 1620 (sometimes written as 1620/21). I have changed these references to reflect the modern calendar.

2. Anonymous [Edward Winslow], *A Relation [Mourt's Relation] or Journal of the Beginnings and Proceedings of the English Plantation Settled at Plimoth in New England* (1622), reprinted in Daniel Mandell, ed., *Early American Indian Documents: Treaties and Laws, 1607–1789*, vol. 19, *New England Treaties, Southeast* (Frederick, MD: University Publications of America, 2003), 26 (hereafter cited as EAID 19).

3. Documents inevitably refer to Native men as *warriors* and groups of warriors as *bands*, which implies that Natives were savages and that their military efforts were at best barely organized; by comparison, European men are *soldiers* only when explicitly engaged in military activity, and they did so in *companies* or other highly organized (i.e., civilized) forms. I reluctantly retain this terminology to avoid unnecessary distractions and because the sources seem to show that it was used by both sides in the war.

4. EAID 19:26.

5. Ibid.

6. There has been a long and often acrimonious debate over whether to use the term "Indians" or "Native Americans." In 1829, the Pequot minister William Apess wrote in his autobiography, *A Son of the Forest*, that Indian "was a word imported for the special purpose of degrading us" and that "the proper term which ought to be applied to our nation, to distinguish it from the rest of the human family, is that of Natives." Yet other Native writings from this period (and even today) use *Indian* rather than *Native*, and surveys of tribes in the United States indicate a preference for the former. To avoid being overly repetitive in this book, I use both "Indians" and "Natives" when not referring to a particular tribe or community. Similarly, I refer to the newcomers as *English* (which is what they usually called themselves), *colonists*, or *settlers*.

7. Early modern England defined sovereignty as "supremacy in respect of power, domination, or rank; supreme dominion, authority, or rule" (see *Oxford English Dictionary*). This was how the English viewed their king or queen, perhaps in theory

along with Parliament: a unitary source of law and political will for the entire nation. That definition does *not* fit how Native communities and sachems (leaders) in the region viewed authority, politics, or law. But the word *is* the best term for the issue that triggered the war. During the war, the Indians who fought alongside the colonists were Christians or members of tribes that for some time had willingly (for their own reasons) embraced colonial dominance. All of these developments went beyond claims to autonomy and reached into the substance of what we today view as the essence of sovereignty: the powers of an independent state with a distinct territory.

CHAPTER ONE: Struggles in New England

1. Phineas Pratt, *A Declaration of the Affairs of the English People that First Inhabited New England* (1662), in EAID 19:35.

2. John Winthrop, "Reasons to Be Considered, and Objections with Answers" (1629), *Winthrop Papers*, vol. 2, *1623–1630*, ed. S. Mitchell (Boston: Massachusetts Historical Society, 1931), 140–42.

3. Nathaniel Morton, *New England's Memoriall* (1669), in *Chronicles of the Pilgrim Fathers*, ed. John Masefield (New York: E. P. Dutton, 1936), 127–28.

4. John Underhill, *Nevvs from America; Or, a New and Experimentall Discoverie of New England* (1638; repr. New York: Da Capo Press, 1971), 42–43.

5. Underhill, *Nevvs from America*, 44.

6. Roger Williams to John Winthrop, 20 August 1637, reprinted in EAID 19:83, 84.

7. Reprinted in EAID 19:152–56.

8. Nathaniel B. Shurtleff, ed., *Records of the Colony of New Plymouth, in New England*, 12 vols. (Boston: W. White, 1855–61), 9:10–12 (hereafter cited as NPR), reprinted in EAID 19:158–60.

9. Samuel Gorton, *Samuel Gorton's Letter to Lord Hyde in Behalf of the Narragansett Sachems* (Providence: Society of Colonial Wars, 1930), reprinted in EAID 19:176–77.

10. Pessicus and Canonicus to Massachusetts, 24 May 1644, in EAID 19:178.

11. Williams to Winthrop Jr., 17 October 1650, reprinted in EAID 19:252.

12. Eaton to Winthrop, reprinted in EAID 19:222.

13. Williams to Massachusetts General Court, 5 October 1654, reprinted in EAID 19:283.

14. NPR 10:158–59, reprinted in EAID 19:294.

15. NPR 10:200; colonial documents, Mass. Archives, 30:85a, 86; NPR 10:268–69.

16. Lion Gardiner, "Lieft Lion Gardener His Relation of the Pequot Warres" (1637), reprinted in Barbara Graymont, ed., *Early American Indian Documents: Treaties and Laws, 1607–1789*, vol. 3, *New York and New Jersey Treaties, 1609–1682* (Frederick, MD: University Publications of America, 1985), 49–51.

17. EAID 19:422.

18. Ibid.

19. Reprinted in Albert Bushnell Hart, ed., *American History Told by Contemporaries*, 5 vols. (New York: Macmillan, 1898), 1:458–60.

CHAPTER TWO: King Philip and Plymouth

1. NPR 5:77–80, reprinted in EAID 19:414.
2. EAID 19:415.
3. Virginia Anderson, *Creatures of Empire: How Domestic Animals Transformed Early America* (New York: Oxford University Press, 2004), 234.
4. NPR 4:164–66, reprinted in EAID 19:405.
5. NPR 5:66–67, reprinted in EAID 19:408.
6. NPR 5:66–67, reprinted in EAID 19:411.
7. Daniel Gookin, *Historical Collections of the Indians in New England*, 1st ser., vol. 1 (Massachusetts Historical Society Collections, 1792), 184–85.
8. Ibid., 186–87.
9. Gookin, *Historical Collections of the Indians*, 191–92, reprinted in EAID 19:391.
10. EAID 19:421.
11. Quoted in Yasuhide Kawashima, *Igniting King Philip's War: The John Sassamon Murder Trial* (Lawrence: University Press of Kansas, 2001), 109–10.
12. Ibid., 110–11.
13. John Easton, *A Relacion of the Indyan Warre* (1858), reprinted in EAID 19:422.
14. Benjamin Church, *Entertaining Passages Relating to Philip's War* (1716), reprinted in EAID 19:417, 418.
15. Quoted in Jenny Hale Pulsipher, *Subjects unto the Same King: Indians, English, and the Contest for Authority in Colonial New England* (Philadelphia: University of Pennsylvania Press, 2005), 101.
16. Ibid., 102.
17. Nathaniel Saltonstall, *The Present State of New England with Respect to the Indian War* (1675), reprinted in *Narratives of the Indians Wars, 1675–1699*, ed. Charles H. Lincoln (1913; New York: Barnes and Noble, 1952), 27.
18. Ibid.
19. John Easton, "A Relaction of the Indyan War," reprinted in *Narratives of the Indians Wars*, 12.
20. Saltonstall, *Present State of New England*, 27.
21. Church, *Entertaining Passages*, reprinted in *So Dreadfull a Judgment: Puritan Responses to King Philip's War, 1676–1677*, ed. Richard Slotkin and James K. Folsom (Middletown, CT: Wesleyan University Press, 1978), 400, 401.
22. Saltonstall, *Present State of New England*, 25.
23. Kyle Zelner, *A Rabble in Arms: Massachusetts Towns and Militiamen during King Philip's War* (New York: New York University Press, 2009).
24. Billerica town records reprinted in Henry A. Hazen, *History of Billerica, Massachusetts* (Boston: A. Williams and Company, 1883), 109–10. Thanks to William Keegan for sending me this reference.

25. Ibid., 29–30.

26. Daniel Gookin, "An Historical Account of the Doings and Sufferings of the Christian Indians in New England, in the Years 1675, 1676, 1677," American Antiquarian Society *Transactions and Collections* 20 (1836), 494, reprinted in EAID 19:445.

CHAPTER THREE: The War Widens

1. Roger Williams, 25 June 1675, reprinted in EAID 19:426–27.

2. William Hubbard, *A Narrative of the Troubles with the Indians in New England . . . to This Present Year 1677* (1677), reprinted in Samuel G. Drake, ed., *The History of the Indian Wars in New England, from the First Settlement to the Termination of the War with King Philip, in 1677* (Roxbury, MA: W. Elliot Woodward, 1865), 1:98.

3. Daniel Gookin, *Historical Collections of the Indians in New England* (Massachusetts Historical Society Collections, 1792), reprinted in EAID 19:391.

4. Hubbard, *Narrative of the Troubles*, 1:120.

5. Ibid.

6. Ibid., 1:123.

7. Ibid., n. 107.

8. Ibid., 2:13.

9. Ibid., 2:100, n. 122.

10. Ibid., 2:100–101.

11. Ingersol quoted in Jenny Hale Pulsipher, *Subjects unto the Same King: Indians, English, and the Contest for Authority in Colonial New England* (Philadelphia: University of Pennsylvania Press, 2005), 75.

12. Hubbard, *Narrative of the Troubles*, 2:22.

13. Daniel Gookin, "An Historical Account of the Doings and Sufferings of the Christian Indians in New England, in the Years 1675, 1676, 1677," American Antiquarian Society *Transactions and Collections* 20 (1836), 444–45.

14. Ibid., 453.

15. Ibid., 463, 483, 492.

16. Ibid., 485, 517.

17. Ibid., 475–77.

18. Ibid., 495.

19. Williams to John Winthrop Jr., 27 June 1675, reprinted in EAID 19:428; Narragansett conference and treaty of 15 July 1675, reprinted in EAID 19:430.

20. NPR 5:357.

21. Quoted in George M. Bodge, *Soldiers in King Philip's War*, 3rd. ed. (Boston, 1906), 180.

22. Hubbard, *Narrative of the Troubles*, 1:140–41.

23. Ibid., 1:140.

24. Ibid., 1:145.

CHAPTER FOUR: Indians Ascendant

1. James Quannapaquait, "Examination and Relation," reprinted in Mary Rowlandson, *The Sovereignty and Goodness of God, with Related Documents*, ed. Neal Salisbury (Boston: Bedford/St. Martins, 1997), 121–22.

2. Daniel Gookin, "An Historical Account of the Doings and Sufferings of the Christian Indians in New England, in the Years 1675, 1676, 1677," American Antiquarian Society *Transactions and Collections* 20 (1836), 486–87.

3. Ibid., 488.

4. Ibid.

5. Ibid., 487.

6. Salisbury, ed., *Sovereignty and Goodness of God*, 68–71.

7. William Hubbard, *A Narrative of the Troubles with the Indians in New England . . . to This Present Year 1677* (1677), reprinted in Samuel G. Drake, ed., *The History of the Indian Wars in New England, from the First Settlement to the Termination of the War with King Philip, in 1677* (Roxbury, MA: W. Elliot Woodward, 1865), 1:169.

8. Noah Newman to John Cotton, 3 March 1676, Curwen Papers, American Antiquarian Society, Worcester, Mass., quoted in Jill Lepore, *The Name of War: King Philip's War and the Origins of American Identity* (Boston: Knopf, 1998), 94 and 283, n. 96.

9. Gookin, "Doings and Sufferings," 494. Printer is named by Drake, *History of the Indian Wars in New England*, 1:171, n. 271.

10. Hubbard, *Narrative of the Troubles*, 1:200.

11. Increase Mather, *A Brief History of the Warr with the Indians in New-England* (Boston, 1676), in *So Dreadful a Judgment: Puritan Responses to King Philip's War, 1676–1677*, ed. Richard Slotkin and James K. Folsom (Middletown, CT: Wesleyan University Press, 1978), 112–13.

12. Ibid.

13. Salisbury, ed., *Sovereignty and Goodness of God*, 105.

14. Hubbard, *Narrative of the Troubles*, 1:207; Nathaniel Saltonstall, *A New and Further Narrative of the State of New-England* (1676), reprinted in *Narratives of the Indians Wars, 1675–1699*, ed. Charles H. Lincoln (1913; New York: Barnes and Noble, 1952), 99.

15. Saltonstall, *New and Further Narrative*, 85.

16. Roger Williams, 25 June 1675, reprinted in EAID 19:446–47.

17. Hubbard, *Narrative of the Troubles*, 1:209.

18. Ibid., 1:79.

19. Saltonstall, *New and Further Narrative*, 98–99.

20. Quoted in Jenny Hale Pulsipher, *Subjects unto the Same King: Indians, English, and the Contest for Authority in Colonial New England* (Philadelphia: University of Pennsylvania Press, 2005), 181.

21. Salisbury, ed., *Sovereignty and Goodness of God*, 105, 106.

22. Quoted in Pulsipher, *Subjects unto the Same King*, 180.

23. Ibid.

24. Gookin, "Doings and Sufferings," 475, 482.

25. Salisbury, ed., *Sovereignty and Goodness of God*, 100.

26. Ibid., 100–101.

27. J. Hammond Trumbull, ed., *The Public Records of the Colony of Connecticut from 1665 to 1678* (Hartford: F. A. Brown, 1852), 426. Thanks to William Keegan for this reference.

28. Mather, *Brief History of the Warr*, 118.

29. Hubbard, *Narrative of the Troubles*, 2:57.

30. Ibid., 2:58–59.

31. Ibid., 2:60.

32. Ibid., 1:182.

33. Saltonstall, *New and Further Narrative*, 91. This is not the same as hung, drawn, and quartered, which under English law was a particularly nasty form of execution reserved for commoners charged with treason. For a description see Geoffrey Robertson, *The Tyrannicide Brief* (New York: Random House, 2005), 13–14.

34. Hubbard, *Narrative of the Troubles*, 2:60.

35. Salisbury, ed., *Sovereignty and Goodness of God*, 123.

36. Gookin, "Doings and Sufferings," 488.

37. Quannapaquait, "Examination and Relation," 124–25.

38. Gookin, "Doings and Sufferings," 508.

39. Hubbard, *Narrative of the Troubles*, 1:184.

40. Gookin, "Doings and Sufferings," 511, 513.

41. Hubbard, *Narrative of the Troubles*, 1:250–51.

42. Benjamin Church, *Entertaining Passages Relating to Philip's War* (1716), reprinted in EAID 19:422, 425.

43. Ibid., 426.

CHAPTER FIVE: Colonists Victorious and Wounded

1. Increase Mather, *A Brief History of the Warr with the Indians in New-England* (Boston, 1676), in *So Dreadful a Judgment: Puritan Responses to King Philip's War, 1676–1677*, ed. Richard Slotkin and James K. Folsom (Middletown, CT: Wesleyan University Press, 1978), 130, 138.

2. Benjamin Church, *Entertaining Passages Relating to Philip's War* (1716), reprinted in EAID 19:442.

3. Mather, *Brief History of the Warr*, 130; William Hubbard, *A Narrative of the Troubles with the Indians in New England . . . to This Present Year 1677* (1677), reprinted in Samuel G. Drake, ed., *The History of the Indian Wars in New England, from the First Settlement to the Termination of the War with King Philip, in 1677* (Roxbury, MA: W. Elliot Woodward, 1865), 1:249.

4. Mattamuck et al. to John Leverett et al., 6 July 1676, in Mary Rowlandson, *The Sovereignty and Goodness of God, with Related Documents*, ed. Neal Salisbury (Boston:

Bedford/St. Martins, 1997), 141; Anonymous, *A True Account of the Most Considerable Occurrences That Have Happened in the Warre between the English and Indians in New-England* (London: Benjamin Billingsley, 1676), 6–7.

5. Mather, *Brief History of the Warr*, 135.

6. William Harris, Papers, *Rhode Island Historical Society Collections* 10 (Providence, 1902), 177–78, reprinted in Charles M. Segal and David C. Stineback, eds., *Puritans, Indians, and Manifest Destiny*, (New York: G. P. Putnam's Sons, 1977), 199–200.

7. Church, *Entertaining Passages*, 443.

8. Ibid., 444.

9. Ibid., 446.

10. Ibid., 447.

11. Ibid., 450.

12. Ibid., 451–52.

13. Ibid., 460.

14. Daniel Gookin, "An Historical Account of the Doings and Sufferings of the Christian Indians in New England, in the Years 1675, 1676, 1677," American Antiquarian Society *Transactions and Collections* 20 (1836), 526.

15. Ibid., 476 n.

16. Hubbard, *Narrative of the Troubles*, 2:63–64.

17. Ibid., 2:142.

18. Ibid., 2:136, 149, 150; Hubbard quoted in Jenny Hale Pulsipher, *Subjects unto the Same King: Indians, English, and the Contest for Authority in Colonial New England* (Philadelphia: University of Pennsylvania Press, 2005), 208.

19. Hubbard, *Narrative of the Troubles*, 2:157.

20. Ibid., 2:172.

21. Ibid., 2:176.

Epilogue

1. *Yamoyden*, quoted in John Gorham Palfrey, "Review of *Yamoyden*," *North American Review* 12 (1820), 485.

2. Sarah Savage, *Life of Philip, the Indian Chief* (Salem: Whipple and Lawrence, 1827), 7–8, 16, 24–25, 29, 32, 51.

3. Lydia Marie Child, *The First Settlers of New England, or, Conquest of the Pequods, Narragansetts and Pokanokets, as Related by a Mother to Her Children, by a Lady of Massachusetts* (Boston, 1829), 13, 65, 272, iii–iv.

4. Jill Lepore, *The Name of War: King Philip's War and the Origins of American Identity* (Boston: Knopf, 1998), 191–92.

5. Quoted in Lepore, *Name of War*, 234.

6. William Apess, *Eulogy on King Philip* (Boston, 1836), in *On Our Own Ground: The Complete Writings of William Apess, a Pequot*, ed. Barry O'Connell (Amherst: University of Massachusetts Press, 1992), 277.

7. "Historical Perspective of the Narragansett Tribe," *Narragansett Indian Tribe* Web site, www.narragansett-tribe.org/history.html (accessed August 11, 2008).

8. "History and Culture," *Mashpee Wampanoag* Web site, http://mashpee wampanoagtribe.com/history2.html (accessed August 11, 2008).

9. "Historical Summary," *Nipmuc Nation* Web site, http://nipmucnation.org/His torical Summary.htm (accessed August 11, 2008).

10. Stephen Webb, *1676: The End of American Independence* (New York: Syracuse University Press, 1995).

SUGGESTED FURTHER READING

There are several books that would be useful to readers seeking more details on the context and events of King Philip's War. Eric B. Schultz and Michael Tougias, *King Philip's War: The History and Legacy of America's Forgotten Conflict* (Woodstock, VT: Countryman Press, 1999), is partly a history of the war that incorporates earlier interpretations and partly a guidebook to the places where significant battles took place; its detailed maps are outstanding. A more analytical work, James D. Drake, *King Philip's War: Civil War in New England, 1675–1676* (Amherst: University of Massachusetts Press, 1999), argues that the war was not between Indians and English but was more of a conflict among different groups of Natives and colonists. Jill Lepore, *The Name of War: King Philip's War and the Origins of American Identity* (Boston: Knopf, 1998), is less a narrative of the war and more an exploration of English, Native, and later American perceptions of the causes, course, and meaning of the conflict, during and after the war. Jenny Hale Pulsipher, *Subjects unto the Same King: Indians, English, and the Contest for Authority in Colonial New England* (Philadelphia: University of Pennsylvania Press, 2005), is probably the best work on the war; it emphasizes sovereignty as the central issue for the English colonists (vis-à-vis the Crown), as well as for tribal leaders, and brilliantly analyzes divisions and union among Natives and colonies at different points in the conflict.

Those who want to delve more deeply into the motives and concerns of colonists and Natives by reading primary sources can find many reprinted in the volumes that I edited in the series *Early American Indian Documents: Treaties and Laws, 1607–1789* (Baltimore: University Publications of America, 2003), including *New England Treaties, Southeast*, vol. 19, and *New England Treaties, North and West*, vol. 20. The best edition of Mary Rowlandson's captivity narrative is Neal Salisbury, ed., *Sovereignty and Goodness of God...by Mary Rowlandson* (1682; Boston: Bedford/St. Martin's Press, 1997). Most of the other works on the war discussed in the epilogue can be readily found in reprints or in the microfilm set *Early American Imprints* (now also available in a digitized collection available by subscription on the Internet). See also Ives Goddard and Kathleen Bragdon, eds., *Native Writings in Massachusett*, 2 vols. (Philadelphia: American Philosophical Society, 1988).

An outstanding resource on Native and English (and French) histories, societies, and cultures throughout New England (and New France) during the seventeenth century is the Internet site *Raid on Deerfield: The Many Stories of 1704*, available at http://1704.deerfield.history.museum/. The site includes biographies, ethnographies, and a cornucopia of maps and images of objects. It is particularly good at distinguishing the various Wabanaki tribes throughout the region and tracking the movement of peoples before and after King Philip's War.

Students exploring the broader causes and context of the war need to begin by understanding Native societies and cultures in the region before English colonization. The best work on this subject is Katherine Bragdon, *Native Peoples of Southern New England, 1500–1650* (Norman: University of Oklahoma Press, 1996). An earlier work is William Cronon's *Changes in the Land: Indians, Colonists, and the Ecology of New England* (New York: Hill and Wang, 1983), a groundbreaking examination of Native economy, society, and land use before and after the English invasion, although it should be read along with Bragdon's book since he depicts a fairly uniform precontact culture in southern New England that seems to reflect Iroquoian influences.

The literature on encounters between Natives and colonists in southern New England before King Philip's War is particularly deep. The most important works include Alden Vaughan, *New England Frontier: Puritans and Indians, 1620–1675* (1965), which tends to present the English perspective; Francis Jennings, *The Invasion of America: Indians, Colonialism, and the Cant of Conquest* (Chapel Hill: University of North Carolina Press, 1975), an angry polemic against the colonists but very strong on the "cold war" with the Narragansetts; James Axtell, *The European and the Indian: Essays in the Ethnohistory of Colonial North America* (New York: Oxford University Press, 1981), which focuses on cultural aspects of the encounter, particularly religion; and Neal Salisbury, *Manitou and Providence: Indians, Europeans, and the Making of New England, 1500–1643* (New York: Oxford University Press, 1982), which is a sensitive and very balanced treatment of the initial encounters from Maine to Connecticut. On the conflict between colonists and Natives over cattle see Virginia DeJohn Anderson, "King Philip's Herds: Indians, Colonists, and the Problem of Livestock in Early New England," *William and Mary Quarterly*, 3rd ser., 51 (1994): 601–24.

Less scholarship exists on northern and western New England. The best work includes *In Search of New England's Native Past: Selected Essays by Gordon Day*, eds. Michael K. Foster and William Cowan (Amherst: University of Massachusetts Press, 1999); Colin Calloway, *Dawnland Encounters: Indians and Europeans in Northern New England* (Hanover, NH: University Press of New England, 1991); sections of Salisbury, *Manitou and Providence*; and chapter forwards in Mandell, *New England Treaties, North and West*. On the Eastern Wabanakis after King Philip's War see Emerson W. Baker and John G. Reid, "Amerindian Power in the Early Modern Northeast: A Reappraisal," *William and Mary Quarterly*, 3rd ser., 61 (2004): 77–106.

The best single work on the Pequot War is Alfred A. Cave, *The Pequot War* (Amherst: University of Massachusetts Press, 1996). The two colonial commanders who recorded their attack on the Mystic fort disagreed about the number of Pequots killed. Cave echoes John Underhill, who put the figure at six hundred, while more recently Peter Hoffer, in *Sensory Worlds in Early America* (Baltimore: Johns Hopkins University Press, 2003), p. 277 n. 40, draws on archeological evidence to argue for the lower figure of four hundred recorded by John Mason. Also of interest is Michael Oberg, *Uncas: First of the Mohegans* (New York: Cornell University Press, 2003).

Many historians have focused on the efforts by John Eliot to convert Natives. A particularly fascinating comparison is between Vaughan's presentation of the Puritan view (in *New England Frontier*), which elevates Eliot, and Jennings's cynical view (in *Invasion of America*) of the missionary as an ineffective Machiavellian profiteer. More balanced interpretations of Eliot and his Indian converts can be found in Richard W. Cogley, *John Eliot's Mission to the Indians before King Philip's War* (Cambridge, MA: Harvard University Press, 1999); Neal Salisbury, "Red Puritans: The 'Praying Indians' of Massachusetts Bay and John Eliot," *William and Mary Quarterly*, 3rd ser., 31 (1974): 30–42; and Harold W. Van Lonkhuyzen, "A Reappraisal of the Praying Indians: Acculturation, Conversion, and Identity at Natick, Massachusetts, 1646–1730," *New England Quarterly* 63 (1990): 396–428.

On the very different Puritan missions on Martha's Vineyard see David Silverman, "Indians, Missionaries, and Religious Translation: Creating Wampanoag Christianity in Seventeenth-Century Martha's Vineyard," *William and Mary Quarterly*, 3rd ser., 62 (2005): 141–74; idem, *Faith and Boundaries: Colonists, Christianity, and Community among the Wampanoag Indians of Martha's Vineyard, 1600–1871* (Cambridge: Cambridge University Press, 2005); and James Ronda, "Generations of Faith: The Christian Indians of Martha's Vineyard," *William and Mary Quarterly*, 3rd ser., 38 (1981): 369–94. Excellent analyses of the many writings by missionaries and Indians are Kristina Bross, *Dry Bones and Indian Sermons: Praying Indians in Colonial America* (Ithaca, NY: Cornell University Press, 2004); and Hilary E. Wyss, *Writing Indians: Literacy, Christianity, and Native Community in Early America* (Amherst: University of Massachusetts Press, 2000). The best work on New England law and Native Americans, particularly with regard to laws addressing religion, is Yasuhide Kawashima, *Puritan Justice and the Indian: White Man's Law in Massachusetts, 1630–1763* (Middletown, CT: Wesleyan University Press, 1986).

There are many other works on King Philip's War in addition to those discussed above. Kyle F. Zelner, *A Rabble in Arms: Massachusetts Towns and Militiamen during King Philip's War* (New York: New York University Press, 2009), connects social and military history to examine how and why primarily poor, rootless, rebellious young men were sent to war. George M. Bodge's *Soldiers in King Philip's War*, 3rd ed. (Boston, 1906) provides an antiquarian narrative that pulls together far more details than any other book on the war and can be used as a source for newer interpretations. Douglas Leach, *Flintlock and Tomahawk: New England in King Philip's War* (New York: Norton, 1958), provides a strong straightforward narrative of the war, albeit primarily from the English point of view. Jennings's *Invasion of America* combined a close reading of the documents with an acerbic cynicism that extended the outrage of the nineteenth-century accounts of the war. For estimates of losses during the war see Sherburn Cook, "Interracial Warfare and Population Decline among the New England Indians," *Ethnohistory* 20 (1973): 20–21. For discussions of English and Native technologies and tactics see in particular Leach, *Flintlock and Tomahawk*, 91–92, 165–66; Drake, *King Philip's War*, esp. 88–89, 124–27; Schultz and Tougias, *King Philip's War*, 125–26, 176–77, 205–6, 226–27, 312; Ian K. Steele, *Warpaths: Invasions of North America* (New York: Oxford University Press, 1994), 96–109; and generally Bodge, *Soldiers in King Philip's War*.

The scholarship on southern New England Indian life after King Philip's War has grown immensely in the last three decades. Much has appeared in collections of articles; particularly significant are Colin G. Calloway and Neal Salisbury, eds., *Reinterpreting New England Indians and the Colonial Experience* (Charlottesville: Colonial Society of Massachusetts and University of Virginia Press, 2003); Colin Calloway, ed., *After King Philip: Presence and Persistence in Indian New England* (Hanover, NH: University Press of New England, 1997); Laurence M. Hauptman and James D. Wherry, eds., *The Pequots in Southern New England: The Rise and Fall of an American Indian Nation* (Norman: University of Oklahoma Press, 1990); and Laurie Weinstein, ed., *Enduring Traditions: The Native Peoples of New England* (Westport, CT: Greenwood Press, 1994). Amy E. Den Ouden, *Beyond Conquest: Native People and the Struggle for History in New England* (Lincoln: University of Nebraska Press, 2005), is particularly strong on the relations between Connecticut authorities and the Pequot and Mohegan tribe during the eighteenth century. My *Behind the Frontier: Indians in Eighteenth-Century Eastern Massachusetts* (Lincoln: University of Nebraska Press, 1996) looks at the development of subregional social and religious networks in the century following the war and examines life within Native communities and the relations between tribes and Massachusetts authorities. More recently I have extended this analysis into the nineteenth century and throughout the region, in *Tribe, Race, History: Native Americans in Southern New England, 1780–1880* (Baltimore: Johns Hopkins University Press, 2008).

Several important works examine particular Native communities and tribes over a broad time span. Silverman's *Faith and Boundaries* moves from the sixteenth into the twentieth century, showing in fascinating detail how Vineyard and Cape Cod Native communities struggled to adapt to the colonial challenge. Jean O'Brien, *Dispossession by Degrees: Indian Land and Identity in Natick, Massachusetts, 1650–1790* (New York: Cambridge University Press, 1997), focuses on how John Eliot's original praying town sought to survive by maintaining its land and examines the kinship connections between that town and other Indian communities in the region. Excellent works on the Narragansetts include Patricia Rubertone, *Grave Undertakings: An Archaeology of Roger Williams and the Narragansett Indians* (Washington, DC: Smithsonian Institution Press, 2001); and Paul R. Campbell and Glenn W. LaFantosie, "Scattered to the Winds of Heaven: Narragansett Indians 1676–1880," *Rhode Island History* 37 (1978): 66–83. Jack Campisi, *The Mashpee Indians: Tribe on Trial* (Syracuse: Syracuse University Press, 1991), is a solid if somewhat brief work on the Mashpee. On Nantucket see various articles by Elizabeth Little published in *Nantucket Algonquian Studies*. On the Wabanakis in the late seventeenth and eighteenth centuries see Kenneth Morrison,

The Embattled Northeast: The Elusive Ideal of Alliance in Abenaki-Euramerican Relations (Berkeley: University of California Press, 1984).

There have also been some important more narrowly focused studies of Native life in southern New England, such as David Silverman, "The Impact of Indentured Servitude on the Society and Culture of Southern New England Indians," *New England Quarterly* 74 (2001): 622–66. Ann Marie Plane, *Colonial Intimacies: Indian Marriage in Early New England* (Ithaca: Cornell University Press, 2000), focuses on family life, marriage, and sex through the eighteenth century. Brian Carroll's dissertation, soon to be completed, is a groundbreaking study of the military service by southern New England Indian men in the century after King Philip's War; the most recent public presentation of his work is "Native American Masculinity in the Provincial Militaries of Massachusetts and Connecticut, 1689–1763," at the 14th Annual Omohundro Institute Conference, Boston, June 7, 2008. A very important work that collects and analyzes Native folklore in the region is William S. Simmons, *Spirit of the New England Tribes: Indian History and Folklore, 1620–1984* (Hanover, NH: University Press of New England, 1986).

After the war, churches became the social and political center of Indian communities in Massachusetts and Plymouth; see Silverman, *Faith and Boundaries*; Mandell, *Behind the Frontier* and *Tribe, Race, History*; and Douglas Winiarski, "A Question of Plain Dealing: Josiah Cotton, Native Christians, and the Quest for Security in Eighteenth-Century Plymouth County," *New England Quarterly* 77 (2004): 368–413. Indian groups in Connecticut and Rhode Island did not embrace Christianity until the 1740s, at which point Samson Occom, Samuel Niles, and several other Native men became ministers and preachers who led their communities and criticized how badly their people were treated by whites. See William and Gertrude Simmons, eds., *Old Light on Separate Ways: The Narragansett Diary of Joseph Fish, 1765–1776* (Hanover, NH: University Press of New England, 1982); and Joanna Brooks, ed., *The Collected Writings of Samson Occom, Mohegan* (New York: Oxford University Press, 2006).

After 1800, William Apess, the Pequot Methodist minister, emerged from this tradition and became the first Indian in America to publish his autobiography. That book and his other works are collected in Barry O'Connell, ed., *On Our Own Ground: The Complete Writings of William Apess, a Pequot* (Amherst: University of Massachusetts Press, 1992). O'Connell's introduction also contains an excellent analysis of how Apess and other New England Indians were affected by race and class. Other works that focus on this topic include my "Shifting Boundaries of Race and Ethnicity: Indian-Black Intermarriage in Southern New England, 1760–1880," *Journal of American History* 85 (1998): 466–501; Ruth Herndon's *Unwelcome Americans: Living on the Margins of Early New England* (Philadelphia: University of Pennsylvania Press, 2002); and John W. Sweet, *Bodies Politic: Negotiating Race in the American North, 1730–1830* (Baltimore: Johns Hopkins University Press, 2003). Both Herndon and Sweet focus on Rhode Island.

INDEX

Page numbers followed by "m" refer to maps; page numbers in *italics* refer to illustrations.